Understanding Our Mind

Thich Nhat Hahn is a Vietnamese Buddhist Zen master, poet, scholar, and human rights activist. In 1967, he was nominated by Martin Luther King, Jr for the Nobel Peace Prize. He is author of more than one hundred books, sixty in English, including *Being Peace*, *Present Moment Wonderful Moment*, and *Calming the Fearful Mind*. He lives at Plum Village, his meditation centre in France, and travels worldwide, leading retreats on the art of mindful living.

Understanding Our Mind

THICH NHAT HANH

HarperCollins *Publishers* India

First published in India by
HarperCollins *Publishers* in 2008

HarperCollins Publishers India, Cyber City, Building 10-A, Gurugram,
Haryana-122002, India
www.harpercollins.co.in

First published by Parallax Press 2006

17

ISBN: 978-81-7223-796-7

This book is the revised paperback edition of Transformation at the Base
The text is a compilation of talks given by Thich Nhat Hanh in Winter Park, Colorado (1989); Malibu, California (1991); Plum Village, France (1992); Key West, Florida (1997); and Regensburg, Germany (1998).
Arnold Kotler, Sister Annabel Laity, and
Marianne Dresser edited the original version.

Thich Nhat Hanhasserts the moral right to be identified
as the author of this book.

Edited by Rachel Neumann
Text design by Gopa & Ted2, Inc.

Printed and bound at
MicroPrints India, New Delhi

MIX
Paper
FSC FSC™ C218906

This book is produced from independently certified FSC® paper to ensure responsible forest management.

HarperCollins Publishers, Macken House, 39/40 Mayor Street
Upper, Dublin 1, D01 C9W8, Ireland

Table of Contents

Introduction

In *Understanding Our Mind*, the Venerable Thich Nhat Hanh shows us how cultivating a deep understanding of our own mind is essential to realizing peace in our world. As we steadfastly care for and meditate on these teachings, they ripen in us and become a source of benefaction for the entire community of living beings. It is an honor to write an introduction to this wonderful and important book.

One of the sources for Thich Nhat Hanh's *Understanding Our Mind* is the Abhidharma literature, the first compilation of commentaries on the Buddha's teachings on philosophy and psychology. As a young Zen student in the late 1960s, I had heard that these commentaries were so highly valued that they had been inscribed on gold tablets, and a great temple had been built to house and protect them. Their importance in the tradition of the Buddhadharma moved me to study them, but reading them seemed so dry, like reading the lists of names in the white pages of a telephone directory. I had trouble finding any life in them, and soon gave up the study.

The depth and poetic intensity of the teachings on mind that constitute this dynamic turning of the Dharma are not easily met or mastered. As part of his study as a novice monk, Thich Nhat Hanh memorized Vasubandu's Twenty Verses and Thirty Verses on Consciousness Only. Memorization may seem difficult and old-fashioned, yet the process enables us to receive these complex teachings in small digestible bites, and to chew them until they are learned by heart and become part of our body and mind. Then meditating on them comes quite naturally because they are deeply woven into the fabric of our conscious activity. Devoting our energy wholeheartedly to the study in this traditional way reveals the deep warmth and vitality of these apparently cold and impenetrable teachings.

Although these teachings on mind are difficult, daunting, and complex, I have found that by going back to them when the time was right, not forcing myself to study them, but approaching them as an amateur, again and again and again, what was originally cold stone broke open, and revealed a great, warm heart, the heart of Buddha's desire that we awaken to the wisdom which lives at the core of these teachings. I have joyously continued to study them up until this day.

Studying these Mahayana teachings on the nature of mind, we realize the mind's true emptiness. When we realize this emptiness, we are free of the conceptual clinging that obscures the true interconnectedness of mind and nature. In this freedom we are able to teach, in creative ways, the intimate and inseparable interdependence of all living and non-living phenomena.

Thich Nhat Hanh's *Understanding Our Mind* is a fresh example of such creative teaching, inspired by and true to the ancients. It conveys the profound wisdom of Buddha's teaching with the simplicity of a warm and peaceful heart.

Tenshin Reb Anderson
Senior Dharma Teacher, Green Dragon Temple
Green Gulch Farm, November 18, 2005

Welcome

THE TWELFTH-CENTURY Vietnamese Zen master Thuong Chieu ("Always Shining") said, "When we understand how our mind works, the practice becomes easy." This is a book on Buddhist psychology, an offering to help us understand the nature of our consciousness.

These Fifty Verses are a kind of road map to the path of practice. The Fifty Verses draw upon the most important streams of Buddhist thought in India, from the Abhidharma teachings of the Pali Canon to later Mahayana teachings such as the Avatamsaka Sutra.[1]

These verses are based on Vasubandhu's Twenty and Thirty Verses, which as a novice monk in Vietnam I studied in Chinese. When I came to the West, I realized that these important teachings on Buddhist psychology could open doors of understanding for people here. So in 1990 I composed the Fifty Verses to continue to polish the precious gems offered by the Buddha, Vasubandhu, Sthiramati, Xuanzang, Fazang, and others. This book was originally published as *Transformation at the Base.* Since its publication, psychologists, therapists, and seekers of all religions have told me how they have found this book helpful in their teachings. With this new edition, I hope to make these teachings accessible to even more readers.

1 Following five hundred years of oral transmission, the Pali Canon was the first written record of the Buddha's teachings. It is also called the *Tipitaka* (Sanskrit: *Tripitaka*), which means "three baskets." The teachings were written down in Ceylon on palm leaves which were then stored in baskets. The three parts of the Canon are: the Sutta-pitaka (Skt., Sutra-pitaka), the original discourses of the Buddha; the Vinaya-pitaka, rules of conduct for the community of monks and nuns; and the Abhidhamma-pitaka (Skt., Abhidharma-pitaka), commentaries on the teachings of the Buddha. The Mahayana movement, which emerged around the first century C.E., was an effort to renew Buddhism and again make it engaged and responsive to the needs of individuals and society. Later on Mahayana texts appeared, rooted in the teachings of the historical Buddha and emphasizing the bodhisattva ideal and the capacity of all beings to be awakened.

You don't have to have a degree in psychology or know anything about Buddhism to enjoy this book. I have tried to present these teachings in a simple way. If, while reading, you don't understand a particular word or phrase, please don't try too hard. Allow the teachings to enter you as you might listen to music, or in the way the earth allows the rain to permeate it. If you use only your intellect to study these verses, it would be like putting plastic over the earth. But if you allow this Dharma rain to penetrate your consciousness, these Fifty Verses will offer you the whole of the Abhidharma teachings in a nutshell.

One could spend an entire lifetime looking deeply into these teachings. Please do not be daunted by their complexity. Go slowly. Try not to read too many pages in one sitting and take the time to absorb each verse and its commentary fully before moving on to the next. Bring mindfulness, kindness, and compassion to your reading of these verses and they will shine light on how the mind works and on the very nature of consciousness.

Fifty Verses on the Nature of Consciousness

Part I. Store Consciousness

One

Mind is a field
in which every kind of seed is sown.
This mind-field can also be called
"all the seeds."

Two

In us are infinite varieties of seeds—
seeds of samsara, nirvana, delusion, and enlightenment,
seeds of suffering and happiness,
seeds of perceptions, names, and words.

Three

Seeds that manifest as body and mind,
as realms of being, stages, and worlds,
are all stored in our consciousness.
That is why it is called "store."

Four

Some seeds are innate,
handed down by our ancestors.
Some were sown while we were still in the womb,
others were sown when we were children.

Five

Whether transmitted by family, friends,
society, or education,
all our seeds are, by nature,
both individual and collective.

Six

The quality of our life
depends on the quality
of the seeds
that lie deep in our consciousness.

Seven

The function of store consciousness
is to receive and maintain
seeds and their habit energies,
so they can manifest in the world, or remain dormant.

Eight

Manifestations from store consciousness
can be perceived directly in the mode of things-in-themselves,
as representations, or as mere images.
All are included in the eighteen elements of being.

Nine

All manifestations bear the marks
of both the individual and the collective.
The maturation of store consciousness functions in the same way
in its participation in the different stages and realms of being.

Ten

Unobstructed and indeterminate,
store consciousness is continuously flowing and changing.
At the same time, it is endowed
with all five universal mental formations.

Eleven

Although impermanent and without a separate self,
store consciousness contains all phenomena in the cosmos,
both conditioned and unconditioned,
in the form of seeds.

Twelve

Seeds can produce seeds.
Seeds can produce formations.
Formations can produce seeds.
Formations can produce formations.

Thirteen

Seeds and formations
both have the nature of interbeing and interpenetration.
The one is produced by the all.
The all is dependent on the one.

Fourteen

Store consciousness is neither the same nor different,
individual nor collective.
Same and different inter-are.
Collective and individual give rise to each other.

Fifteen

When delusion is overcome, understanding is there,
and store consciousness is no longer subject to afflictions.
Store consciousness becomes Great Mirror Wisdom,
reflecting the cosmos in all directions.
Its name is now Pure Consciousness.

Part II. Manas

Sixteen

Seeds of delusion give rise
to the internal formations of craving and afflictions.
These forces animate our consciousness
as mind and body manifest themselves.

Seventeen

With store consciousness as its support,
manas arises.
Its function is mentation,
grasping the seeds it considers to be a "self."

Eighteen

The object of manas is the mark of a self
found in the field of representations
at the point where manas
and store consciousness touch.

Nineteen

As the ground of wholesome and unwholesome
of the other six manifesting consciousnesses,
manas continues discriminating.
Its nature is both indeterminate and obscured.

Twenty

Manas goes with the five universals,
with mati of the five particulars,
and with the four major and eight secondary afflictions.
All are indeterminate and obscured.

Twenty-One

As shadow follows form,
manas always follows store.
It is a misguided attempt to survive,
craving for continuation and blind satisfaction.

Twenty-Two

When the first stage of the bodhisattva path is attained,
the obstacles of knowledge and afflictions are transformed.
At the tenth stage, the yogi transforms the belief in a separate self,
and store consciousness is released from manas.

Part III. Mind Consciousness

Twenty-Three

With manas as its base
and phenomena as its objects,
mind consciousness manifests itself.
Its sphere of cognition is the broadest.

Twenty-Four

Mind consciousness has three modes of perception.
It has access to the three fields of perception and is capable
of having three natures.
All mental formations manifest in it—
universal, particular, wholesome, unwholesome, and indeterminate.

Twenty-Five

Mind consciousness is the root of all actions of body and speech.
Its nature is to manifest mental formations, but its existence is not continuous.
Mind consciousness gives rise to actions that lead to ripening.
It plays the role of the gardener, sowing all the seeds.

Twenty-Six

Mind consciousness is always functioning
except in states of non-perception,
the two attainments,
deep sleep, and fainting or coma.

Twenty-Seven

Mind consciousness operates in five ways—
in cooperation with the five sense consciousnesses
and independent of them,
dispersed, concentrated, or unstably.

PART IV. SENSE CONSCIOUSNESSES

Twenty-Eight

Based on mind consciousness,
the five sense consciousnesses,
separately or together with mind consciousness,
manifest like waves on water.

Twenty-Nine

Their field of perception is things-in-themselves.
Their mode of perception is direct.
Their nature can be wholesome, unwholesome, or neutral.
They operate on the sense organs and the sensation center of the brain.

Thirty

They arise with the
universal, particular, and wholesome,
the basic and secondary unwholesome,
and the indeterminate mental formations.

Part V. The Nature of Reality

Thirty-One

Consciousness always includes
subject and object.
Self and other, inside and outside,
are all creations of the conceptual mind.

Thirty-Two

Consciousness has three parts—
perceiver, perceived, and wholeness.
All seeds and mental formations
are the same.

Thirty-Three

Birth and death depend on conditions.
Consciousness is by nature a discriminatory manifestation.
Perceiver and perceived depend on each other
as subject and object of perception.

Thirty-Four

In individual and collective manifestation,
self and nonself are not two.
The cycle of birth and death is achieved in every moment.
Consciousness evolves in the ocean of birth and death.

Thirty-Five

Space, time, and the four great elements
are all manifestations of consciousness.
In the process of interbeing and interpenetration,
our store consciousness ripens in every moment.

Thirty-Six

Beings manifest when conditions are sufficient.
When conditions lack, they no longer appear.
Still, there is no coming, no going,
no being, and no nonbeing.

Thirty-Seven

When a seed gives rise to a formation,
it is the primary cause.
The subject of perception depends on the object of perception.
This is object as cause.

Thirty-Eight

Conditions that are favorable or non-obstructing
are supporting causes.
The fourth type of condition
is the immediacy of continuity.

Thirty-Nine

Interdependent manifestation has two aspects—
deluded mind and true mind.
Deluded mind is imaginary construction.
True mind is fulfilled nature.

Forty

Construction impregnates the mind with seeds of delusion,
bringing about the misery of samsara.
The fulfilled opens the door of wisdom
to the realm of suchness.

Part VI. The Path of Practice

Forty-One

Meditating on the nature of interdependence
can transform delusion into enlightenment.
Samsara and suchness are not two.
They are one and the same.

Forty-Two

Even while blooming, the flower is already in the compost,
and the compost is already in the flower.
Flower and compost are not two.
Delusion and enlightenment inter-are.

Forty-Three

Don't run away from birth and death.
Just look deeply into your mental formations.
When the true nature of interdependence is seen,
the truth of interbeing is realized.

Forty-Four

Practice conscious breathing
to water the seeds of awakening.
Right View is a flower
blooming in the field of mind consciousness.

Forty-Five

When sunlight shines,
it helps all vegetation grow.
When mindfulness shines,
it transforms all mental formations.

Forty-Six

We recognize internal knots and latent tendencies
so we can transform them.

When our habit energies dissipate,
transformation at the base is there.

Forty-Seven

The present moment
contains past and future.
The secret of transformation
is in the way we handle this very moment.

Forty-Eight

Transformation takes place
in our daily life.
To make the work of transformation easy,
practice with a Sangha.

Forty-Nine

Nothing is born, nothing dies.
Nothing to hold on to, nothing to release.
Samsara is nirvana.
There is nothing to attain.

Fifty

When we realize that afflictions are no other than enlightenment,
we can ride the waves of birth and death in peace,
traveling in the boat of compassion on the ocean of delusion,
smiling the smile of non-fear.

PART I

Store Consciousness

According to the teachings of Manifestation Only Buddhism, our mind has eight aspects or, we can say, eight "consciousnesses."[2] The first five are based in the physical senses. They are the consciousnesses that arise when our eyes see form, our ears hear sounds, our nose smells an odor, our tongue tastes something, or our skin touches an object. The sixth, mind consciousness (*manovijñana*), arises when our mind contacts an object of perception. The seventh, *manas*, is the part of consciousness that gives rise to and is the support of mind consciousness. The eighth, store consciousness (*alayavijñana*), is the ground, or base, of the other seven consciousnesses.[3]

2 Both Vijñanavada and Yogachara were early Mahayana Buddhist schools based on the study of the nature of consciousness. *Vijñana* means literally "mind" or "consciousness." The school is more commonly referred to as the Mind Only or Consciousness Only school. This name is often misunderstood as a kind of idealism, however, so throughout this book I will refer to it as the Manifestation Only (Vijñaptimatra) school. Yogachara means "application of yoga" or meditation, particularly the meditative practices of the perfections (*paramita*), the essential qualities of a bodhisattva.

3 All schools of Buddhism recognize a basic consciousness from which "mental formations" (*chitta-samskara*) arise. The Tamrashatiya school called it "stream of constituents of existence" (*bhavangashrota*), the stream of being, the ground for samsara and rebirth. The Manifestation Only school also described consciousness as always continuous, like a stream of water. Master Tâng Hôi, the first Dhyana (Zen) master in Vietnam, compared the mind to an ocean ("ocean-mind"). Everything we see, hear, smell, taste, touch, feel, or think flows into the ocean of our mind like thousands of rivers. In the Sarvastivada school, the term "root, or base, consciousness" (*mulavijñana*) was used. In the Thirty Verses, Vasubandhu used the Sarvastivada terms "root consciousness" and "transforming consciousness." Original Buddhism used the words *chitta* (sometimes called *chitt- raja*, "mind-king"), *manas*, and *vijñana* interchangeably for "mind." By the time of the development of Manifestation Only Buddhism, each of these three terms had its own sphere of meaning. "Chitta" referred to store consciousness—the root, or basis, of consciousness. Phenomena (*dharma*) that arise from store

Verses One through Fifteen are about store consciousness. Store consciousness has three functions. The first is to store and preserve all the "seeds" (*bija*) of our experiences. The seeds buried in our store consciousness represent everything we have ever done, experienced, or perceived. The seeds planted by these actions, experiences, and perceptions are the "subject" of consciousness. The store consciousness draws together all these seeds just as a magnet attracts particles of iron.

The second aspect of store consciousness is the seeds themselves. A museum is more than the building, it is also the works of art that are displayed there. In the same way, store consciousness is not just the "storehouse" of the seeds but also the seeds themselves. The seeds can be distinguished from the store consciousness, but they can be found only in the storehouse. When you have a basket of apples, the apples can be distinguished from the basket. If the basket were empty, you would not call it a basket of apples. Store consciousness is, at the same time, both the storehouse and the content that is stored. The seeds are thus also the "object" of consciousness. So when we say "consciousness," we are referring to both the subject and the object of consciousness at the same time.

The third function of store consciousness is as a "store for the attachment to a self."[4] This is because of the subtle and complex relationship between manas, the seventh consciousness, and the store consciousness. Manas arises from store consciousness, turns around and takes hold of a portion of store consciousness, and regards this grasped part as a separate, discrete entity, a "self." Much of our suffering results from this wrong perception on the part of manas, and it is the subject of our in-depth study in Part II of this book.

---

consciousness are called "mind functions" (*chaitasika*). The Avatamsaka Sutra uses the term "mind only" (*chitta matrata*). Later, in the Lankavatara Sutra, the terms "manifestation only" (*vijñapti matrata*) and "consciousness only" (*vijñana matrata*) were introduced.

4 Although terms like "ability to store," "object stored," "all the seeds," and "store for the attachment to a self" were first used in the Manifestation Only school of Mahayana Buddhism, the basis of their meaning was already present in teachings of Original and Many-Schools Buddhism. (See Afterword.)

I

The Mind Is a Field

Mind is a field
in which every kind of seed is sown.
This mind-field can also be called
"all the seeds."

THE PRIMARY FUNCTION of store consciousness is to store and preserve all the seeds. One name for store consciousness is *sarvabijaka,* the totality of the seeds. Another is *adana,* which means to maintain, to hold, not to lose. Maintaining all the seeds, keeping them alive so that they are available to manifest, is the most basic function of store consciousness.

Seeds (bija) give phenomena the ability to perpetuate themselves. If you plant a seed in springtime, by autumn a plant will mature and bear flowers. From those flowers, new seeds will fall to the earth, where they will be stored until they sprout and produce new flowers. Our mind is a field in which every kind of seed is sown—seeds of compassion, joy, and hope, seeds of sorrow, fear, and difficulties. Every day our thoughts, words, and deeds plant new seeds in the field of our consciousness, and what these seeds generate becomes the substance of our life.

There are both wholesome and unwholesome seeds in our mind-field, sown by ourselves and our parents, schooling, ancestors, and society. If you plant wheat, wheat will grow. If you act in a wholesome way, you will be happy. If you act in an unwholesome way, you will water seeds of craving, anger, and violence in yourself and in others. The practice of mindfulness helps us identify all the seeds in our consciousness and with that knowledge we can choose to water only the ones that are the most beneficial. As we cultivate the seeds of joy and transform seeds of suffering in ourselves, understanding, love, and compassion will flower.

2

Every Kind of Seed

In us are infinite varieties of seeds—
seeds of samsara, nirvana, delusion, and enlightenment,
seeds of suffering and happiness,
seeds of perceptions, names, and words.

OUR STORE CONSCIOUSNESS contains every kind of seed. Some seeds are weak, some strong, some large, some small, but all are there—the seeds of both samsara and nirvana, of suffering and happiness. If a seed of delusion is watered in us, our ignorance will grow. If we water the seed of enlightenment, it will grow and our wisdom will flourish.

Samsara is the cycle of suffering, our dwelling place when we live in ignorance. It is difficult to remove ourselves from this cycle. Our parents suffered and they transmitted the negative seeds of this suffering to us. If we don't recognize and transform the unwholesome seeds in our consciousness, we will surely in turn pass them on to our children. This constant transmission of fear and suffering drives the cycle of samsara. At the same time, our parents also transmitted seeds of happiness to us. Through the practice of mindfulness, we can recognize the wholesome seeds within ourselves and in others and water them every day.

Nirvana means stability, freedom, and the cessation of the cycle of suffering. Enlightenment does not come from outside; it is not something we are given, even by a Buddha. The seed of enlightenment is already within our consciousness. This is our Buddha nature—the inherent quality of enlightened mind that we all possess, and which needs only to be nurtured.

In order to transform samsara into nirvana, we need to learn to look deeply and see clearly that both are manifestations of our own consciousness. The seeds of samsara, suffering, happiness, and nirvana are already in our store consciousness. We need only to water the seeds of happiness, and avoid watering the seeds of suffering. When we love someone, we try to recognize the positive seeds within them and water those wholesome seeds with our kind words and deeds. The seeds of happiness grow stronger when they are watered, while the seeds of suffering diminish in strength because we are not watering them with unkind words and deeds.

Our store consciousness also contains seeds generated from our perceptions. We perceive many things, and the objects of these perceptions are then stored in our store consciousness. When we perceive an object, we see its "sign" (*lakshana*). The Sanskrit word "lakshana" also means "mark," "designation," or "appearance." The sign of a thing is the image that is created by our perception (*samjña*) of it. Suppose we see a wooden platform supported by four legs. That image becomes a seed within our consciousness. The name we assign to this image, "table," is another seed. "Table" is the object of our perception. We, the perceiver, are the subject. The two are linked every time we perceive the object we have named as a "table," or even when we simply hear the word "table," our image of a table manifests in our mind consciousness.

Buddhism identifies three pairs of signs of phenomena. The first pair is the universal and the particular sign of something. When we look at a house, the sign, or image, "house" is initially universal. The universal sign "house" is like its generic label. Now, you can buy generic food in some supermarkets. Instead of color images and brand names, the label on a can of corn, for example, displays simply the word "corn" in black type on a plain white wrapping. The universal sign of an object is like that.

Using our discriminative mind, however, we soon perceive thousands of details about each house—the brick, wood, nails, and so on, that are specific to it. These specifics are the particular sign of a house. The house can be seen as a whole—its universal sign—or as a combination of its parts, its particular sign. Everything has both a universal and a particular nature.

Connected to this, the second pair of signs is unity and diversity. Our notion of house is an idea of unity. All houses are part of the designation "house;" there is no difference between one house and another. But the universal notion of "house" does not show us any individual house, which is unique in its particulars. There are countless variations of houses, and that is the nature of diversity. When we look at any phenomenon (*dharma*), we should be able to see unity in the diversity, and diversity in the unity. While the first sign distinguishes between a universal house and a particular house, the second sign is about how we distinguish between different particular houses.

The third pair of signs is formation and disintegration. A house may be in the process of being built, but at the same time it is also in the process of disintegrating. Even though the wood is new and the house is not yet completely built, already the moisture or dryness of the air is beginning to weather it. Looking at something that is beginning to take form, we should already be able to see that it is also in the process of disintegrating as well.

Meditation training is designed to help us learn to see both aspects of each pair of signs. We see the whole when we are looking at the parts, and each part when we are looking at the whole. When a carpenter looks at a tree, he can already envision a house, because he has been trained in constructing a house from the material of the tree. He is seeing both the universal and particular aspects of the tree. Through mindfulness we train ourselves to see all six signs—universal and particular, unity and diversity, formation and disintegration—whenever we perceive a single sign, a specific object. This is the teaching of interbeing.

We assign names and words, or "appellations," to the objects of our perception, such as "mountain," "river," "Buddha," "God," "father," "mother." Every name we've assigned to a phenomenon, every word we've learned, is stored as a seed within our consciousness. The seeds give rise to other seeds in us, called "images." When we hear the name of something, an image arises in our consciousness, and we then take that image to be reality. As soon as we hear someone say the words "New York," for example, we immediately touch the seeds of the image of New York we have in our store consciousness. We picture the Manhattan skyline or the faces of people we know there. These images may differ from the current reality of New York, however. They may be entirely creations of our imagination, but we cannot see the boundary between reality and our erroneous perceptions.

We use words to point to something—an object or a concept—but they may or may not correspond to the "truth" of that thing, which can only be known through a direct perception of its reality. In our daily life we rarely have a direct perception. We invent, imagine, and create perceptions based on the seeds of the images that we have in our store consciousness. When we fall in love, the image of our beloved that we hold in our minds may be quite different from the actual person. You might say that we end up marrying our false perception rather than the person herself.

Erroneous perceptions bring about much suffering. We feel certain that our perceptions are correct and complete, yet often they are not. I know a man who suspected that his son was not his own but was the child of a neighbor who had visited his wife often. The father was too proud and ashamed to tell his wife or anyone else about his suspicion. Then one day a visiting friend remarked how much the boy looked like his father. At that moment, the man realized that the boy was indeed his own son. Because he had held onto this wrong perception, the family endured much pain for many years. Not only these three people but everyone around them also suffered because of this wrong perception.

It is very easy to confuse our mental image, our sign of something, with its reality. The process of mistaking our perceptions for reality is so subtle that it is very difficult to know that it is going on, but we must try not to do this. The way to avoid this is mindfulness. We practice meditation to train the mind in direct perception, in correct perception. When we meditate, we look deeply into our perceptions in order to find out their nature and to discover the elements that are correct and the elements that are incorrect.

If you are not mindful, you will believe that your perceptions, which are based on prejudices that have developed from the seeds of past experiences in your store consciousness, are correct. When we have a wrong perception and continue to maintain it, we hurt ourselves and others. In fact, people kill one another over their different perceptions of the same reality.

We live in a universe filled with false images and delusions, yet we believe that we are truly in touch with the world. We may have a deep respect for the Buddha and believe that if we were to meet him in person, we would bow before him and attend all of his teachings. But, in reality, we may have already met the Buddha in our own town and not had the slightest wish to even go near him, because he didn't conform to our image of what a Buddha is supposed to look like. We are certain that a Buddha appears with a halo, wearing beautiful robes. So when we meet a Buddha in ordinary clothes, we do not recognize him or her. How could a Buddha wear a sport shirt? How could a Buddha be without a halo?

There are so many seeds of wrong perception in our consciousness. Yet we are quite sure that our perception of reality is correct. "That person hates me. He will not look at me. He wants to harm me." This may be nothing more than a creation of our mind. Believing that our perceptions are reality, we may then act out of that belief. This is very dangerous. A wrong perception can create countless problems. In fact, all our suffering arises from our failure to recognize things as they are. We should always ask ourselves, humbly, "Am I sure?" and then allow space and time for our perceptions to grow deeper, clearer, and more stable. In medical practice these days, physicians and caregivers are reminded by each other to not be too sure of anything. "Even if you think you are certain, check it again," they urge each other.

3

Nothing Is Lost

Seeds that manifest as body and mind,
as realms of being, stages, and worlds,
are all stored in our consciousness.
That is why it is called "store."

BEFORE SOMETHING MANIFESTS, we say that it doesn't exist. Once we are able to perceive it, then we say that it exists. But even though a phenomenon is unmanifested, it is always there, as a seed in our consciousness. Our body, our mind, and the world are all manifestations of the seeds that are stored in our consciousness.

This verse refers to several Buddhist concepts on the various modes of existence of living beings, which will be explained in greater detail in later chapters. Briefly, the "realms of being" (*dhatu*) are the three realms of desire (*kamadhatu*), form (*rupadhatu*), and non-form (*arupadhatu*). The realm of desire is where we touch the presence of craving, anger, arrogance, and delusion. Beings in this realm suffer a lot because they are always running after things. When we choose to live simply and abandon some of our craving, we are in the realm of form. In this realm we suffer less and can experience a little happiness. In the third realm, the formless realm, materiality is absent. Only energy is present, and this energy manifests as our mind, our anger, our suffering, and so forth. Life continues, but there is no perception of form.

The realm of desire, together with the four levels of the realm of form and the four levels of the realm of non-form, make up nine stages of being. (The levels of each realm and the stages are described in greater detail in Chapter Nine.) When you have not been liberated from your misconceptions, you can be caught in the realms of desire, form, and non-form. Early

Buddhist texts talk about these three realms of samsaric existence as being like a "house on fire." The three realms are burning, and it is we who light the fire through the false perceptions of our consciousness.

The purpose of Buddhist practice is to transform the suffering of these realms and stages. If we practice looking deeply at the nature of craving, we will become emancipated from the realm of desire and begin to dwell in the realm of form, which is a higher realm. Looking even more deeply, we can lessen our attachment to form and begin to dwell in the realm of non-form. In the realm of non-form, suffering still exists because all wrong perceptions have not yet been removed and many desires are still dormant in the depth of our consciousness. It is possible to touch all three realms in the present moment, around us and within us.

Each realm of being is a result of the collective consciousness of those dwelling there. If our world is a peaceful, happy place, it is because of our collective consciousness. If it is on fire, we are co-responsible for that. Whether a place is pleasant or unpleasant always depends upon the collective consciousness of its inhabitants. If five or six people practice and attain the fruits of joy, peace, and happiness, and if these people then go out and establish a practice center, manifesting their happiness in a setting in which others can participate, then they have established a small "pure land." The realms of being all come from our mind, manifesting from the seeds that are stored in our consciousness.

Seeds also manifest as two kinds of worlds. The first is the world of sentient beings—humans, animals, and vegetal species. Human society and the societies of animal and vegetal species all arise in the collective consciousness. The second is the instrumental world, where the so-called non-sentient beings dwell—mountains, rivers, air, the earth, the ozone layer, and the like. The instrumental world is the world of nature and it, too, is the creation of our collective consciousness. Our store consciousness manifests and holds the seeds of all these worlds, and they all function in accord with certain laws and rhythms.

All formations are a manifestation of our consciousness. In the *Standard Verses on the Eight Consciousnesses*, Xuanzang says, "[Consciousness] receives, impregnates, maintains, and preserves the body-basis and the Instrumental World."[5] Consciousness receives and is impregnated with all the experiences and perceptions that come to us through seeing, hearing, smelling, tasting, and touching. Our experiences and perceptions then become seeds in our store consciousness. This is called "impregnation" (*vasana*). Everything we learn enters our store consciousness, leaves its "scent," and is preserved there. We may think we have forgotten something, but nothing that the store consciousness receives is lost; everything is stored there, unmanifested, until the conditions for its manifestation are present.

5 An English translation by Ronald Epstein of Xuanzang's *Pa-shih Kuei-chu Sung (Verses on the Structure of the Eight Consciousnesses)* can be found at: http://online.sfsu.edu/~rone/Buddhism/Yogacara/BasicVersescontents.htm.

4

Transmission

Some seeds are innate,
handed down by our ancestors.
Some were sown while we were still in the womb,
others were sown when we were children.

SOME SEEDS are received by us during our lifetime, in the sphere of our experience. Some seeds, however, were already present when we were born, in the sphere of innate seeds. At the time of our birth, these innate seeds were already present within our consciousness—seeds of suffering and happiness that were transmitted to us by many generations of our ancestors. Many of our abilities, mannerisms, and physical features, as well as our values, were handed down to us by our ancestors. During our lifetime, when the conditions for their manifestation are favorable, some of these seeds will manifest. Some will not manifest in our own lifetime but we will transmit them to our children, who will then transmit them on to their children. Perhaps a few generations later, during the lifetime of one of our great-grandchildren, the conditions will be favorable and certain of those transmitted seeds will then manifest.

The science of genetics shows that the "blueprint" for the characteristics of our body and mind come from many generations of our ancestors. Scientists conducting experiments with rats found that it might take seven generations before a distinct characteristic reappears. So when we practice mindfulness, we are not practicing for ourselves alone but also for our ancestors and for the countless generations to follow. All these generations are already within us. The experiences of our ancestors, as well as infinite time and infinite space, are already contained within the consciousness of even a tiny embryo. When we understand this, we feel a tremendous responsibility toward each embryo.

If we set aside one day a week to learn about and practice peace, joy, and happiness, during those twenty-four hours we will bring happiness to our ancestors and to future generations. If we allow a week to pass without practicing, not only do we experience the loss of an opportunity for joy but it is also a loss for our ancestors, our children, and their children. When we are liberated from suffering and realize peace and joy, our ancestors also realize peace and joy, and future generations will receive from us seeds of peace and joy.

The seeds that have been handed down to us can be described as "habit energies." You may think you don't know how to sing, but the seeds of singing, passed down from your grandmother who could sing, are already within you. Under the right circumstances, not only will you remember how to sing, you will find yourself enjoying it. When you begin to practice singing, those seeds that are weak from lack of use will spring forth and grow strong. Seeds like these are largely innate. All that is needed for them to flower are favorable conditions.

The same is true of enlightenment. When we first learn about the teachings on awakening, we think these teachings are new to us. But we already have the seed of awakening within us. Our teacher and our friends on the path only provide the opportunity for us to touch that seed and help it grow. When the Buddha realized the path of great understanding and love, he remarked, "How amazing that all living beings have the basic nature of awakening, yet they don't know it. So they drift on the ocean of great suffering, lifetime after lifetime."[6] There are many healthy and wholesome seeds already within our consciousness. With the help of a teacher and a Sangha, a community of practitioners, we can come back to ourselves and touch them. Having access to a teacher and a Sangha are the favorable conditions that allow our seed of awakening to grow.

In every cell of our body, in our store consciousness, are seeds that have been transmitted to us by every generation of our ancestors. The "impreg-

6 *Buddhacarita* XIV, 50 and 51.

nation" of our consciousness takes place even before we are born, while we are still in our mother's womb. As soon as we are conceived, we begin receiving more seeds. Every perception, every joy, and every sorrow of our mother and our father penetrates us as a seed. The greatest gift new parents can give their children is their own happiness. If parents live happily with each other, the child will receive seeds of happiness. But if the parents get angry at each other and make each other suffer, all those negative seeds will penetrate the store consciousness of the baby.

Bringing a new life into the world is a serious matter. Doctors and therapists spend up to ten years to get a license to practice. But anyone can become a parent without any training or preparation. We need to create an "Institute of the Family" where young people, before they get married, can go for one year to practice looking deeply into themselves to see what kinds of seeds in them are strong and what kinds of seeds are weak. If the positive seeds are too weak, prospective parents need to learn ways to water them in order to make them stronger. If the negative seeds are too strong, they should learn ways to transform them, to live in a way that those seeds will not be watered so much.

One year of preparation for getting married and starting a family is not too much to ask. Mothers-to-be can learn how to sow seeds of happiness, peace, and joy, and avoid sowing unhealthy seeds in their babies' store consciousness. Fathers-to-be also need to be aware that the way they act sows seeds in the store consciousness of their unborn child. A few severe words, a reprehending look, or an uncaring action—the baby in the womb receives it all. The store consciousness of the fetus receives everything that is going on in the family. A thoughtless word or deed might stay with a child the rest of her life.

At this institute, young men and women can also get in touch with their ancestors and parents to help them know who they are—their strengths and weaknesses—and help them to learn how to handle their own seeds. This is an important project. Young parents should keep a record of the joys and difficulties they have during the time before and after conception and a record of the suffering, happiness, and the significant events during the life of the child, from age one to ten. The child may forget most of the things that happen during this period, but if parents can tell their children these things, it will be very helpful to them later, after they have grown up and when it is time for them to go and study at the institute.

We have received seeds of suffering from our parents. Even if we are determined to do the opposite of what our parents did, if we don't know how to practice and transform these seeds, we will do exactly the same as they did. During our lifetime, we continue to receive seeds from our parents. Their joys and their suffering continue to penetrate us. If our father says something that makes our mother happy, we receive seeds of happiness. If our father says something that makes our mother cry, we receive seeds of suffering.

You can protect your child from the beginning. Living mindfully is very important during the nine months that the baby is growing in the womb. And after the baby is born, parents should continue to be mindful. The baby may not understand the words of your conversation, but your voices convey your feelings. If you say something with love, the baby will feel it. If something is said in irritation, the child will receive it. Don't think that because your baby is in the womb or still very tiny, he does not understand. Whatever is in the atmosphere of the family goes into the baby's store consciousness. If the atmosphere at home is heavy, the baby will feel it.

Many children cannot bear the heavy atmosphere of their homes, and they hide in the bathroom or another room in order not to hear the words that create wounds in their hearts. Sometimes children get sick because of the way their parents talk to each other. They may then be afraid of adults and those in authority the rest of their lives. I have seen babies who play naturally and happily when no adults are in the room, but as soon as the door opens and an adult walks in, they become limp and silent. The seeds of fear in them are already so great. Suffering begins before we are born. And some seeds are present in our store consciousness even before that, transmitted to us by our ancestors.

Children are so tender and vulnerable. That is why, as parents, we must do our best not to say anything that will cause suffering for our little boy or little girl. We know that the mark of that suffering will be with them their whole life. Many children are abused physically and emotionally by their parents, and because of this they suffer all of their lives. Mindful living—the awareness that our children are a continuation of ourselves—is extremely helpful. Looking deeply and living mindfully, we see that our children are our continuation. They are nothing other than ourselves. If we have suffered because of our parents, we know that the negative seeds of our parents are already within us. If we aren't capable of recognizing those seeds in ourselves and practicing to transform them, we will do to our children exactly what our parents have done to us. This cycle of suffering can be ended through the practice of mindful living.

To understand how the seeds in our store consciousness are transmitted across generations, the Buddha proposed looking into the transmission of the physical body. Your body has been transmitted to you by your father, your mother, and your ancestors; you have received this transmission; and your body is the object of this transmission. The three elements in this process of transmission are: the one who transmits, the object transmitted, and the recipient of the transmission.

The Buddha invites us to look into the nature of each thing and find the emptiness of its transmission. We ask ourselves the question: What did my father transmit to me? The answer is: He transmitted himself to me. The object transmitted is nothing other than himself, and I really am the continuation of my father. I am my father. Our ancestors are in us. Sometimes they manifest in the way we smile, speak, or think. Then we ask: Who is the recipient of the transmission? Is it a separate entity? No. The recipient of the transmission is the object of both the transmission and of the transmitter. The object of transmission is one with the transmitter.

When you penetrate the truth of the emptiness of transmission, you can realize that you *are* your father. You can no longer say, "I don't want to have anything to do with my father; I'm too angry." In fact, you are the continuation of your father. The only thing you can do is reconcile yourself with him. He is not out there, apart from you—he is in you. Peace is possible only with this knowledge and reconciliation.

5

Individual and Collective Seeds

Whether transmitted by family, friends,
society, or education,
all our seeds are, by nature,
both individual and collective.

OUR SOCIETY, country, and the whole universe are also manifestations of seeds in our collective consciousness. Plum Village, the monastery and practice center where I live in France, is a manifestation of consciousness. Those of us who live there have a collective manifestation of Plum Village that we hold in common, but each of us also has a personal manifestation of Plum Village in our own mind. The Plum Village of Sister Doan Nghiem is not the same as the Plum Village of Brother Phap Dang. Plum Village has its individual and collective faces.

If you say that Plum Village is both an objective and a subjective reality, that is not exactly correct. You may think there is an objective reality of Plum Village that you will be able to grasp some day, though you have only experienced the subjective reality of Plum Village in your own consciousness. But what you call "objective" also arises from your consciousness. Our consciousness includes both individual and collective, subjective and objective. Yet we continue to believe that consciousness is one thing, and that there is an outer "objective" reality, apart from consciousness, upon which our image of Plum Village is formed.

We compare, struggle, and wonder how to let go of our personal, subjective view and arrive at an objective recognition of things. We want to be directly in touch with the reality of the world. Yet the objective reality we think exists independently of our sense perceptions is itself a creation of collective consciousness. Our ideas of happiness and suffering, beauty and ugliness are reflections of the ideas of many people. Collective consciousness is not just the consciousness of three or four people but of hundreds or thousands of people. Some things start out as creations of individual consciousness and then become part of collective consciousness.

Our store consciousness includes both individual and collective consciousness. What is considered fashionable, for example, is a creation of the collective consciousness of a society. You believe that you have your own notion of beauty, but if you look deeply you will see that it has been formed from the notions of many other people. When you shop for a necktie, you think it is you who chooses the tie. But the moment you see a tie that aligns with the seeds in your store consciousness, the necktie chooses you. You think you have exercised your freedom of choice, but the choice was already made a long time ago.

When a painting sells for millions of dollars, this is because our collective consciousness has deemed it valuable. A child may look at the painting and say that it's ugly or worthless. Our appreciation of the painting reflects not only our personal idea of beauty but the idea of beauty held by society and by our ancestors. Our enjoyment of food is the same. To me, pickled mustard greens are delicious. My ancestors ate them, and the seeds in my consciousness have the habit energy of enjoying them also. To you, pickled mustard greens may not be tasty at all. Tasty or awful, beautiful or ugly, depends on the seeds in our consciousness, both individual and collective.

Democracy and other political structures are creations of collective consciousness. The stock market, the value of the dollar, and the price of gold are also the products of collective consciousness. People who work in the stock exchange are always calculating, guessing, buying and selling. That is how the monetary value of stocks, gold, and the dollar increase or decrease. These calculations and deductions create a chain reaction that brings about a collective understanding, and sometimes this speculation brings incalculable suffering. The ups and downs of the stock market are manifestations of our collective fears and hopes. Heaven, hell, our nation's Constitution, and the goods we consume in daily life—all are manifestations of our collective consciousness.

No seed in our consciousness is one hundred percent innate or one hundred percent transmitted. It is not that some seeds are purely individual and some are purely collective. If you are a good musician, the seed of that ability is considered to be your individual seed. But if we look deeply we can see its collective nature as well. You might have received this ability from your ancestors, from your teachers, or even from listening to the radio. The seed is yours, it exists in your store consciousness, but it has been sown there by the happiness and suffering, the abilities and weaknesses, of everyone with whom you've been in contact.

Each seed in our store consciousness is both individual and collective at the same time. Nothing is completely collective or completely individual. The individual can be seen in the collective, and the collective in the individual. The collective is made of the individual, and the individual is made of the collective. This is the nature of interbeing.

In fact, the distinction between innate and transmitted seeds, between individual and collective, is provisional. These distinctions are established in order to help us better understand on an intellectual level seemingly opposite concepts, so that we can work with them in our practice. When our practice matures, when we see the nature of interbeing of everything, we no longer need these distinctions.

Therefore, we need to transcend ideas of individual and collective; everything has both elements in it, the collective and the individual inter-are. A bus driver's optic nerve may seem to be individual, specific and important only to him, but the quality of his optic nerve may affect the safety of many other people. We may believe that we are nonviolent, but there is the seed of violence in us that has been watered by television, newspapers, or by what we have seen or experienced. If we look deeply, we will see that this seed has both an individual and a collective nature at the same time.

During meditation retreats, we practice mindful breathing, smiling, and walking. A retreat creates a particular environment that is conducive to mindfulness. That is the collective nature of such an event. By walking mindfully, paying attention to our breathing, and practicing smiling, we are cultivating our individual well-being. But just as the collective is in the individual, the individual also has an effect on the collective. The moment we take a peaceful step, the world changes. The moment we smile, not only do we change a little but those with whom we come in contact also change a little. The individual always has an effect on the collective, and the collective always has an effect on the individual. All seeds in our store consciousness have this dual nature, individual and collective. It is important to remember this when we are practicing to cultivate our wholesome seeds and not to water our unwholesome seeds.

For this reason, we need to associate with those who water seeds of joy in us. It's not that we want to discriminate against those who suffer, but when our own wholesome seeds are still weak, we need to associate with friends who water the seeds of peace, health, and happiness in us. When the seeds of peace and happiness have become more solidly established within us, we will be able to be of more help to those who suffer. We need to know when we are strong enough to help, or we may be overwhelmed by the difficult seeds in the other person.

At a retreat center, there are always some people in severe mental pain. A Dharma teacher has the responsibility to sit and listen to them, to open her heart and be fully present in order to help. But if the teacher does not practice mindfulness of the dual and permeable nature of individual and collective consciousness, she may receive more suffering than she can endure and she won't be able to help others. If she does not practice mindfulness while she is listening, the suffering of the other person will only water the seeds of suffering in her. Being a Dharma teacher does not give us the capacity to do things beyond our strength. Teachers have to limit the number of suffering people they see or they may collapse.

The same is true for psychotherapists. You have to open your heart to understand the suffering of your client and find ways to help. But, after helping someone, you need to be in contact with what is refreshing and healing in yourself and in the world around you. When you have reached your capacity to absorb suffering, you must not see any more clients until you have restored your own seeds of health and peace. This is the way to sustain the work of helping.

You don't have to be a Dharma teacher or a psychotherapist to help others. We all spend time listening to our friends. After hearing their pain, we can practice walking meditation or do some joyful task. This will give us a good chance to become fresh and clear again, strong enough to help again in the future. If we open our hearts freely but don't know our limitations, our own seeds of agitation will be watered and we will become overwhelmed. We need to continue to practice watering the healthy seeds in our consciousness. Many people who want to help feel they don't have the right to rest because there are so many people who need their help. But if they don't rest, if they don't restore themselves, not only will they lose their own sense of peace and joy, they will no longer be a resource for others.

Sigmund Freud, the father of modern psychology, had an idea of the unconscious that in some ways corresponds to the Buddhist concept of the store consciousness. But the unconscious is just a tiny part of the store consciousness. The seventh consciousness, manas, is more or less equivalent to the notion of "ego" in the psychoanalytic school developed by Freud. What Freud called the "superego" has some affinity with the sixth consciousness, mind consciousness. Carl Jung, who was influenced by Freud, went further and said that the emotions and experiences of suffering and happiness in our minds also reflect the collective consciousness. Jung drew some of his ideas from Tibetan Buddhism. Many psychotherapists since Jung have adopted his way of thinking.

No doubt Buddhist psychology will continue to have an influence on Western psychology. The methods of healing psychological illness will gradually be deeply influenced by the Manifestation Only teachings. During retreats I have offered to psychotherapists, we practice conscious breathing, sitting meditation, and walking meditation together, recognizing and embracing our pain, and these practices become a part of our lives. This is the best offering Buddhism can make to Western psychotherapy.

When we speak of collective consciousness, we tend to think of a modern day consciousness, changing with the issues and fashions of the day. But the collective aspect of seeds in our consciousness also comes from our ancestors and from all those who have gone before us. The seeds in our consciousness contain the experiences, ideas, and perceptions of many people throughout space and time. Our consciousness is infused with the collective consciousness throughout time and space.

So where is our store consciousness? It is within each cell of our body, and it is also outside of our body. Each cell in our body possesses all the characteristics, elements, experiences, joy, and suffering of many generations of ancestors. In fact, our genes are like the seeds in our store consciousness.

Just as consciousness is both individual and collective, each cell of our body is unique and also contains within it the genetic map of our entire body. Science has now become able to replicate, through cloning, an entire living being from only one cell of the body.

The ideas of "individual" and "collective," "inside" and "outside," can be transcended. Inside is made of outside. When we touch our own skin, we touch the water, heat, air, and earth that are within us. At the same time, we know that these elements also exist outside our bodies. Looking deeply, we realize that the sun is also our heart. If the heart inside of our body stops functioning, we will die right away. In the same way, if the sun, our second heart, stops shining, we will also die right away. The whole cosmos is our body, and we are also the body of the entire cosmos.

6

The Quality of the Seeds

The quality of our life
depends on the quality
of the seeds
that lie deep in our consciousness.

WHETHER WE HAVE HAPPINESS or not depends on the seeds in our consciousness. If our seeds of compassion, understanding, and love are strong, those qualities will be able to manifest in us. If the seeds of anger, hostility, and sadness in us are strong, then we will experience much suffering. To understand someone, we have to be aware of the quality of the seeds in his store consciousness. And we need to remember that he is not solely responsible for those seeds. His ancestors, parents, and society are co-responsible for the quality of the seeds in his consciousness. When we understand this, we are able to feel compassion for that person. With understanding and love, we will know how to water our own beautiful seeds and those of others, and we will recognize seeds of suffering and find ways to transform them.

When someone comes to us for guidance, we need to look deeply into that person in order to see the seeds that are lying deep in their consciousness. Offering only some general teaching or advice will not really help them. If we look deeply, we can recognize the quality of the seeds in that person. This is called "observing the circumstances." Then we can recommend a specific path of practice to nurture the positive seeds and to transform the negative ones.

If we feel that there is someone whom we cannot help, it is only because we have not yet looked deeply enough into his or her circumstances. Everyone has some seeds of happiness. In some people they are weak, while in others they are strong. You might be the first person in many years to touch your friend's seeds of happiness. Helpfulness lies in our ability to see and to water these wholesome seeds. If we see only greed, anger, and pride, we have not yet looked deeply enough.

The French philosopher Jean-Paul Sartre said, "Man is the sum of his acts." Each of us is a collection of our actions, and our actions are both the cause and result of seeds in our store consciousness. When we do something, our action is a cause (*karma-hetu*). When it bears a result, it is an effect (*karma-phala*, "action-fruit"). Every act we make through our body, speech, and mind sows seeds in our consciousness, and our store consciousness preserves and maintains these seeds.

There are three kinds of action: mind action, or thought; speech action; and bodily action. Thought precedes the other two kinds of action. Even though we may not yet have done anything or spoken in a harmful way, our harmful thinking can be enough to make the universe tremble. The effect of our words on others is called speech action. Whether our words bring suffering or happiness depends on our own happiness, on the quality of the seeds in our store consciousness. Bodily action refers to our physical acts, whether harmful or helpful. The seeds of all three kinds of action are held in the eighth consciousness, the store consciousness.

Many Buddhist practitioners recite the Five Remembrances daily. The fifth is, "My actions are my only true belongings. I cannot escape the consequences of my actions. My actions are the ground on which I stand." When we die and transform from one form of being to another, and leave behind our possessions and those we love, only the seeds of our actions will go with us. Consciousness does not hold on only to mind actions. The seeds of our speech actions and bodily actions also travel with our store consciousness from this world to another.

To know whether someone is happy, you only have to look at the seeds in his store consciousness. If there are strong seeds of unhappiness, anger, discrimination, and delusion, he will suffer greatly, and it is likely that through his actions he will water these unwholesome seeds in others. If his seeds of understanding, compassion, forgiveness, and joy are strong, not only is he capable of true happiness but he will be able to water the seeds of happiness in others. Our daily practice is to recognize and water the wholesome seeds in ourselves and others. Our happiness and the happiness of others depend on it.

There are four practices associated with Right Effort, part of the Noble Eightfold Path that the Buddha taught as the path to liberation.[7] The first practice of Right Effort is to prevent the unwholesome seeds that have not yet manifested from manifesting. "Unwholesome" means not conducive to liberation. If these harmful seeds are watered, they will manifest and grow stronger. But if we embrace them with our mindfulness, sooner or later they will weaken and return to our store consciousness.

The second practice of Right Effort is to help the unwholesome seeds that have already arisen in our mind consciousness to return to store consciousness. Again, mindfulness is the key. If we can recognize when a harmful seed has manifested in our mind consciousness, we will be able to avoid being caught by it. The third practice of Right Effort is to find ways to water the wholesome seeds in our store consciousness that have not yet arisen, to help them manifest in our mind consciousness. And the fourth practice is to maintain as long as we can the mental formations that have already arisen from wholesome seeds on the level of our mind consciousness. (We will talk more about how mind consciousness works later in this book.)

Our practice of Right Effort is nourished by joy. If we water the seeds of happiness, love, loyalty, and reconciliation every day, we will feel joyful, and this will encourage these seeds to stay longer, to strengthen. It is important to know how to sustain our practice. A story about the Buddha illustrates this.

The Buddha asked the monk Sona, "Is it true that before you became a monk, you were a musician?" Sona replied that it was so. The Buddha asked, "What happens if the string of your instrument is too loose?"

"When you pluck it, there will be no sound," Sona replied.

"What happens when the string is too taut?"

"It will break."

7 The Noble Eightfold Path is Right View, Right Thinking, Right Speech, Right Action, Right Livelihood, Right Diligence (or Right Effort), Right Mindfulness, and Right Concentration. See Thich Nhat Hanh, *The Heart of the Buddha's Teaching* (Berkeley, CA: Parallax Press, 1998), chaps. 9–16.

"The practice of the Way is the same," the Buddha said. "Maintain your health. Be joyful. Do not force yourself to do things you cannot do."[8]

In order to sustain our practice, we need to know our physical and psychological limits and find a balance between effort and rest. We shouldn't force ourselves in the practice. The practice should be pleasant, joyful, nourishing, and healing. At the same time, we should be careful not to lose ourselves in sensual pleasures. The fourfold practice of Right Effort lies in the Middle Way between these two extremes.

8 *Vinaya Mahavagga Khuddaka Nikaya* 5.

7

Habit Energies

The function of store consciousness
is to receive and maintain
seeds and their habit energies,
so they can manifest in the world, or remain dormant.

THE SEEDS that we receive from our ancestors, friends, and society are held in our consciousness, just as the earth holds the seeds that fall upon it. Like the seeds in the earth, the seeds in our store consciousness are hidden from us. We are seldom in contact with them. Only when they manifest in our mind consciousness do we become aware of them. When we feel happy, we may believe that there is no seed of anger in us. But as soon as someone irritates us, our seed of anger will make itself known.

Habit energy is an important term in Buddhist psychology. Our seeds carry the habit energies of thousands of years. The Sanskrit term for habit energy, vasana, means "to permeate," "to impregnate." If you want to make jasmine tea, you pick jasmine flowers, put them in a box together with the tea, close it tightly, and leave it for several weeks. The fragrant jasmine penetrates deeply into the tea leaves. The tea will then smell of jasmine, because it has absorbed the perfume of the jasmine blossoms. Our store consciousness also has a strong capacity to receive and absorb fragrances.

This perfuming of our consciousness affects our patterns of seeing, feeling, and behaving. The seeds in our consciousness manifest not only in a psychological form but also as the objects of our perception—mountains, rivers, other people. Because of habit energies, we are not able to perceive things as they truly are. We interpret everything we see or hear in terms of our habit energy. If you crumple a sheet of paper, it is difficult to make it lie flat again. It has the habit energy of being crumpled. We are the same.

When we meet a person, what we really meet is our own habit energy, and it prevents us from seeing anything else. Perhaps when we first met this person, we had a negative reaction to him. We formed a habit energy of how we relate to him on the basis of that, and we continue to relate to him that way. Every time we look at him, we see the same old person, even if he has changed completely. Our habit energies keep us from being able to perceive the reality of the present moment.

We are influenced by the actions and beliefs of our parents and of society. But our reactions to things have their own patterns and we are caught in these patterns. Our habit energies are the fruit of our behavior, formed by our reactions to things and also by our environment. When a person is brought up in a certain environment, a habit energy is formed. Many children today have the habit energy of watching TV. They are unhappy when they are brought somewhere where there is no television. One boy, when he came to Plum Village and discovered that there was no television, wanted his mother to take him away. We convinced him to stay for half a day, and during that time many other children played with him. After a few hours, he agreed to stay longer. He ended up staying for three weeks. He discovered that he could be happy without television.

That is the good news. It is possible for us to change our habit energies. And in fact, in order to transform we must change them. Even though we may have the best intention to transform ourselves, we will not be successful unless we work on our habit energies. The easiest way to do this is with a Sangha, a group of people who practice mindfulness together. If we put ourselves in an environment where we can practice deeply with other people, we will be able to alter our habit energies. Through the practice of mindfulness, we can identify the seeds in us and recognize the habit energies that go along with them. With mindfulness, we can observe our habit energies and begin to transform them.

If our families and friends are unstable, they will also affect our consciousness. That is why it is important to choose carefully who we spend time with. When we talk with someone who is unhappy, our store consciousness will receive the seeds of her suffering. If we aren't careful to maintain our own wholesome seeds during the conversation, her suffering will water the seeds of suffering in us and we will feel exhausted.

The practice of mindfulness allows us to create new, more functional habit energies. Suppose that when we hear a certain phrase, we grimace. It's not that we want to make a face, it just happens automatically. To replace this old habit energy with a new one, every time we hear that phrase we breathe consciously. At first conscious breathing requires effort. It doesn't yet come naturally. If we continue to practice, however, conscious breathing will become a habit energy. We form any new habit in the same way. When you first begin brushing your teeth after meals, you might forget sometimes. After a while it becomes a habit, and not brushing is uncomfortable.

Some habit energies are very difficult to transform. Smoking is a habit energy that is hard to give up. Mindfulness is the key. Whenever we are smoking, we practice mindfulness in order to know that we are smoking. Our mindfulness of this habit energy will grow deeper every day, and we will see that we are destroying our lungs. Then we will see the link between our lungs, our health, and the people we love. We realize that looking after ourselves is also looking after our loved ones. Then we will make the decision to take care of our body—for their sake as well as our own. Mindfulness encourages these kinds of insights.

Drinking is another habit energy. Perhaps every time we feel sad we drink a glass of wine in order to forget our sadness. With mindfulness, each time we raise our glass we say, "I know that I am drinking a glass of wine." When our mindfulness is stronger, we will be able to say, "I know that I am sad," when we drink wine. As our insight grows and we see more deeply the sadness behind our habit energy of drinking wine, we will be able to begin to transform the seeds of sadness in ourselves.

Happiness can also be a habit energy. When we practice walking meditation, every step we take brings us peace and joy. When we first begin to practice walking meditation, we may have to make an effort. We are not yet skilled at it. But one day we begin to feel peace and joy quite naturally. We wonder, "Why was I always in such a hurry?" Once we feel at ease with walking meditation and other ways of moving mindfully, they become a wholesome habit.

Though there are positive habit energies, it seems that negative habits are established more quickly than positive ones. At school our children are exposed to both good and bad habits, but they seem to learn the bad ones right away. It takes time for a young person to learn to appreciate Shakespeare, but it doesn't take long at all to learn to drink alcohol. When you teach something to a child, you may have to repeat it again and again, so that the seed will be planted solidly in the child's consciousness. When you paint a wall, the first coat is not enough. You have to paint over it a second and a third time. This is how we learn.

We have to recognize, embrace, and transform our negative habit energies and train ourselves to have more positive habit energies. I was fortunate that early in my life I learned the good habit of practicing sitting meditation every day to calm myself and to cultivate more stability, solidity, and freedom. Many of us now have learned the habit of returning to our breathing and smiling every time we hear the bell of mindfulness. These positive habits need to be cultivated, because our negative habits always push us to do and say things that bring suffering to ourselves and others.

8

Fields of Perception

Manifestations from store consciousness
can be perceived directly in the mode of things-in-themselves,
as representations, or as mere images.
All are included in the eighteen elements of being.

WHEN SEEDS in our store consciousness manifest themselves in our mind consciousness, either we perceive them directly or we do not perceive them directly. There are three modes, or fields, of perception: direct, as representation, and as mere images. According to the Manifestation Only teachings, the way we perceive reality has everything to do with our happiness and suffering.

The first field of perception is the perception of things-in-themselves, perceiving directly without distortion or delusions.[9] This is the only one of the three modes of perception that is direct. This way of perceiving is in the realm of noumena, or suchness. Suchness (*tathata*) means "reality as it is." Another name for the Buddha is *Tathagata*, which means "the one who has come from suchness and goes to suchness." Everything—a leaf, a peb-

9 "Things-in-themselves" is a term from the German philosopher Immanuel Kant (1724–1804). Kant proposed that the mind's contribution is one of four groups of categories through which we order the contents of our experience: quantity, quality, relation, and modality. These categories are without content and only prescribe the structure for objects of possible experience. Space, for example, is not something that is external to us but is only a structure in the mind that relates objects to one another. It is the mind's active contribution that gives meaning to the external material of our experience. Whether things really are the way they appear to us is something we can never know, because all our knowledge is prestructured through the filter of the mind. This is the basis for Kant's famous distinction between the unknowable noumenon, or thing-in-itself, and the phenomenon, or thing-as-it-appears.

ble, you, me—comes from suchness. Suchness is the ground of our being, just as water is the ground of being of a wave.

Are we capable of touching reality-in-itself? The Buddhist teachings say that we can. A flower can be the manifestation of the world of suchness, if we perceive it directly. It all depends on our mode of perception whether we touch the suchness of the flower or only an image of it that our minds have created. Our perceptions rarely reach the mode of things-in-themselves, however. We usually perceive things in the other two modes, as representations or mere images.

When we fall in love, for example, we usually fall in love with an image we have of our beloved. We cannot eat, sleep, or do anything because this image in us is so strong. Our beloved is beautiful to us, but our image of him may actually be far from the reality. We don't realize that the object of our perception is not the reality-in-itself but an image we have created. After we marry and live with our beloved for two or three years, we realize that the image that we held on to and stayed awake at night thinking about was largely false. The object of our perception, our image of our beloved, belongs to the second mode of perception, the mode of representations. Our consciousness manifests an image of the object and we love that image. The image we love may have nothing to do with the person-in-himself. It is like taking a photograph of a photograph.

We are unable to reach the mode of perceiving things-as-they-are-in-themselves because our distorted image is a "representation," not a direct perception. It is not one hundred percent part of the world of suchness because it contains only a small part of the reality it is based on. The person we love is not a real person, but an image created by our consciousness. This false perception can create suffering. Sitting in the car next to our spouse, we completely ignore her because we think that we already know everything about her and that there is nothing interesting to learn about her anymore. We are caught in these kinds of feelings and perceptions. Sometimes anger and hatred replace love, but these perceptions do not correspond to the realm of things-in-themselves, either.

In this way, we may live with someone for thirty years and still be unable to comprehend the truth of that person. Perhaps our present image of her is closer to the world of things-in-themselves than the image we had thirty years ago, but it is still an image—it still belongs to the world of representations. Scientists have acknowledged that they don't even know what a speck of dust is. Looking deeply into an electron, we bow our heads in awe. And yet here is a human being sitting next to us and we think we already know everything about her. We hate or love depending on images we ourselves create. Most of our perception, longing, and aversion occur in the mode of representations or in the third mode of perception, the mode of mere images. We, too, must always continue to learn. We need to look closely at the things we think belong to the world of things-in-themselves and see whether they are really only representations or mere images.

The third mode of perception is the field of mere images. In this mode of perception, what we perceive are purely images. If while walking in the street you see a dog, your perception of it belongs to the realm of representations. If you go home and dream of the dog, your dream-image is in the field of mere images. In our dreams we "see" people, mountains, and rivers. All of these belong to the realm of mere images. When we practice visualization, we are also using images drawn from this third mode of perception.

All images, whether we perceive them in the mode of representations or the mode of mere images, are false. They are not a direct perception of things-in-themselves. According to the Manifestation Only teachings, we live much more in the world of representations and mere images than in the world of things-in-themselves. Our consciousness rarely touches reality. We imprison ourselves in our own distorted images of reality.

Suppose you are walking in a field at dusk. In the path ahead you see a long, curving shape that you "recognize" as a snake. You become frightened. Then someone shines a flashlight on the snake and you discover that it is in fact only a piece of rope. The fear you felt was the result of a wrong perception. Seeing a piece of rope, you touched the image of a snake in your store consciousness. You did not touch the realm of reality-in-itself, but instead the realm of mere images.

Much of the suffering we experience every day comes from our false perceptions, based on fear and ignorance. Hindus and Muslims, Palestinians and Israelis, have a lot of fear because of their images of one another. Because they are dwelling in the realm of representations, they continue to make themselves and others suffer. We live day in and day out in the realm of representations, full of errors and discriminations, and we suffer because of it.

The first five consciousnesses—the sense consciousnesses of eye, ear, nose, tongue, and body—are capable of touching the realm of things-in-themselves, especially when they contact their objects of perception without the participation and intervention of mind consciousness. When mind consciousness gets involved, however, there will always be some thinking and imagination, and the image brought to it by one of the sense consciousnesses will become distorted. When we see a table, what we perceive as a "table" belongs to the field of representations, because our perception has a lot of mind consciousness in it. We think of a table as something that we can put things on. Termites see it as a source of food. Whether we view the table as food or a surface, our perception of it is not occurring in the realm of things-in-themselves. Anything touched in the realm of things-in-themselves by a sense consciousness and then processed by mind consciousness becomes a representation. Yet even our mind consciousness can touch the realm of things-in-themselves from time to time. When we have a strong intuition, our mind consciousness is in touch with the realm of suchness. Intuition is a form of knowing that is not based in thinking and imagining.

Consciousness has the job of manifesting and differentiating our perceptions through these three modes of perception. To manifest in consciousness, both a subject and an object of perception are needed. While Western philosophy regards subject and object as opposites, the Manifestation Only teachings say that they are two aspects of the same reality.

Our store consciousness is responsible for manifesting all three modes of perception: things-in-themselves, representations, and mere images. All three fields of perception are included in the eighteen elements of being, which are made up of the six sense bases, their six objects of perception, and the resulting six consciousnesses. The sense organs (*indriya*)—the eyes, ears, nose, tongue, body, and mind—are also called gates (*ayatana*) because all that we perceive enters through them. These sense organs are the bases for contact with the sense objects of form, sound, smell, taste, tactile objects, and objects of mind. The sense gates and their corresponding objects (*vishaya*) bring about the sense consciousnesses. When the eyes are in contact with a form, the resulting awareness of form is called eye consciousness. Similarly, when the other five sense bases come in contact with their objects of perception, their corresponding consciousnesses are brought about. The objects of mind are thinking, imagination, and ideas. The result is mind consciousness.

Dharmas, objects of mind, are found in all three worlds: the world of things-as-they-are, the world of representations, and the world of mere images. The eighteen elements of being are the fields in which existence is possible. Someone asked the Buddha, "What is the world? How can we talk about everything that is?" He replied, "Everything that exists can be found in the eighteen elements. Outside of these, nothing can be found." The eighteen elements are a manifestation of our individual and collective consciousnesses. All objects of our perception are included in these eighteen elements.

As you read this book, the sheet of paper in your hand is in the realm of reality-in-itself. Whether we can touch its true nature is the question. We may think we are perceiving the sheet of paper as it is, but we probably aren't. We are caught by the habit of seeing and thinking determined by ideas like self and other, inside and outside, this and that, beginning and end. When we divide the universe into categories we can only touch the field of representations, not the field of things-in-themselves. Even when we actually touch the paper—the object of our perception—with our fingers and our eyes, the thing that appears to our perception is not the paper's suchness, but a representation.

We are capable of reaching the field of things-in-themselves, the world of suchness, but because we think and discriminate we don't usually perceive things as they truly are. The nature of our mind is obstructed (*parikalpita*). This means that we build a world full of illusion for ourselves because of the distorted way we perceive reality. Meditation is to look deeply in order to arrive at reality—first the reality of ourselves and then the reality of the world. To get to that reality, we have to let go of the images we create in our consciousness and our notions of self and other, inside and outside. Our practice is to correct this tendency to discriminate and think dualistically, so that reality will have a chance to reveal itself.

9

Ripening and Emancipation

All manifestations bear the marks
of both the individual and the collective.
The maturation of store consciousness functions in the same way
in its participation in the different stages and realms of being.

ONLY WHEN THE SEEDS hidden in the depths of our consciousness mature and manifest in our mind consciousness do we become aware of them. When our anger and sorrow are dormant, we cannot see them. But when we become angry, our face reddens, our voice rises, the seed of our anger has ripened and we notice it. The seeds of anger were there before we became angry, but they were hidden in our store consciousness. If we had said, "I am not angry," this wouldn't have been correct. The seeds of anger were there even though they had not yet manifested.

Manifestation (*vijñapti*) is an important term. What is manifested is a function of consciousness, and it is also perceived by consciousness. All the manifestations we see in the eighteen elements of being are in the three fields of things-in-themselves, representations, and mere images. And all manifestations bear the mark of both the individual and the collective. Sometimes they are more individual than collective, sometimes the reverse. The full moon is a manifestation of both our collective and individual store consciousness. Everyone has the right to enjoy the moon and in this way it is collective. But many of us do not have time to touch the moon. The moon is closer to some people than to others.

We can create paradise or hell in our own minds. What conditions do you need to be truly happy? If those conditions are never realized, will you suffer for the rest of your life? Or could you manage to be happy even without them? We have many conditions for happiness, but we rarely benefit from them. Please write down some conditions for happiness that are available to you right now. Could you organize your life so that you are able to recognize them when they are present? Try to arrange your life to make these conditions for happiness available. Don't ignore or destroy them. When there is something you don't like, how can you make it more acceptable? Please reflect on these questions.

All manifestations of phenomena arise from our store consciousness. Store consciousness manifests itself into mental formations and physical formations—our sense organs of eyes, ears, nose, tongue, and body and their objects of forms, sounds, smells, tastes, and tactile sensations. Store consciousness also manifests as the three fields of perception—the realm of things-in-themselves or suchness, which we can touch every time we have the insight of interbeing, nonduality, impermanence, and nonself; the realm of representations, where we live our daily lives caught in a way of thinking that is contrary to the principles of nonduality and interbeing; and the realm of mere images, the world of dreams, imagination, and recollection.

All these manifestations bear the marks of the individual and the collective. All manifestations of the natural world, such as trees, grass, mountains, and rivers; all physical manifestations, including our own body and the bodies of others; and all psychological manifestations, such as anger, sadness, fear, and anxiety—all are manifestations with both individual and collective aspects. There is no manifestation of a phenomenon that is purely individual or purely collective.

Looking into the seed of anger in us, we can see its individual and its collective nature. Our anger has roots in our experiences with our parents, teachers, friends, and our own lives. The sun shines for everyone, but this is not just a purely collective manifestation. Sunshine also has an individual aspect—it is different for you than for me. If I am planning a picnic, I want the sun to shine all day. A farmer, however, may wish for rain to water his crops. In Southeast Asia, people long for clouds to cover the hot sun and cool the air. In North America, a hot, sunny day makes people happy. These are examples of the sun's individual aspects.

When we light a candle, many places are illuminated—the immediate area around the candle, then the area a little further away, then even further away. When we light a second candle, it also projects the same three areas of light. And in each of these areas of light, the light of the other candle enters with varying intensity. Once we've lit the second candle, there is not a single area of light that comes from only one candle. There is always the light of the other candle in it. The different areas of light do not have only an individual manifestation; they also have a collective manifestation.

Because all manifestation has both an individual and collective aspect, it would not be correct to say that a young man in prison bears the whole responsibility for his crime. He is the product of his family, his schooling, and society. If we look deeply, we may find that when he was younger, his parents often fought and caused each other and their child to suffer. Perhaps he was abused. Lacking love, lacking education, he tried to forget himself in drugs. With drugs, his ability to make good choices diminished even further. Committing a crime was the result.

Looking deeply, we see that the conditions for this young man's actions did not arise only from his own mind and experiences. All of us bear some responsibility for creating the conditions that led him into the cycle of crime and addiction. If we only condemn or punish him, it will not help. People use drugs because they are in pain and want to run away from life. Putting someone who is suffering like this in prison is not the way to solve the problem. There has to be love and understanding, some means of bringing him back into life, offering him joy, clarity, and purpose.

Our fear, sorrow, anger, and happiness also bear the mark of the individual and the collective. Our brain is not just individual. The way we think, perceive, and create reflects the collective consciousness. And our collective consciousness reflects and also helps manifest the world we perceive and in which we live.

Maturation is another way of describing store consciousness. You put all the seeds into one container—the store consciousness—and wait until every perception, feeling, and mental formation is manifested through maturation. Each perception, feeling, and mental formation bears the mark of both individuality and collectivity. The Sanskrit word for maturation, *vipaka*, can be translated as "ripening." A seed always needs the right amount of time and the right conditions in order to ripen and bring forth fruit. When it matures, a seed transforms into a form of being that is the true manifestation of its qualities: an orange blossom produces an orange. The blossom needs the proper time and conditions in order to become an orange that we can eat. Similarly, an act needs time in order to ripen. Our actions, our *karma*—what we say, think, and do—need time to mature. When they manifest, they manifest in participation with other consciousnesses.

The ripening of phenomena happens in three ways:

1) **Ripening at different times.** Suppose we pick a custard apple, a bunch of bananas, and a jackfruit and put them away. The custard apple will ripen first, then the bananas, and finally the jackfruit. The seeds that our parents, grandparents, and friends sow and water in us always ripen sooner or later. There is no need to ask, "Why am I not transformed when I have studied so many teachings of the Buddha? Why do I still not feel peace and joy when I have practiced walking meditation so much?" Each seed ripens in its own time. Our practice is simply to water the positive seeds in ourselves. We should have confidence that if we continue to water a certain seed, it will germinate and grow.

2) **Ripening of different varieties.** An unripe banana becomes a ripe banana—it can never become a ripe custard apple.

3) **Ripening and changing.** When something ripens, many of its aspects change completely. An unripe orange is green and sour. A ripe one is orange and sweet.

To sow a seed is an action-as-cause (karma-hetu). When the action-as-cause ripens, it becomes an action-as-result, or action-fruit (karma-phala). Suppose your coworker yells at you and makes you lose confidence in yourself. Because of this action, a harmful seed is sown not only in your consciousness but in his as well. Compared to the seed planted by a previous courageous action of his, this seed is less significant. But there are now two seeds in your coworker's consciousness, one constructive and one destructive. When these two seeds ripen, they will take him to a place that represents an average of the weight of both actions.

Maturation means the conclusion of all the actions-as-cause upon their ripening. When we look deeply, we see that our own psychology and physiology, our happiness and our suffering, are all actions-as-result in the present moment of actions-as-cause from the past. Looking back, we can see the past actions that were sown as seeds in our store consciousness. Thanks to the wholesome seeds sown by our teachers, friends, parents, and others, we can now enjoy peace and joy as we practice walking meditation. Looking in the present, we see that if we continue to water and sow these wholesome seeds, our peace and joy will be even greater in the future.

The way we are now is the sum of action A plus action B. When we look deeply at our body and mind, we see the level of happiness, ease, and freedom in ourselves. Then we slowly shed light on what we have done in the past, the people who have helped us, the things we have put into practice that today bring us this sense of happiness, ease, and freedom. And we also look into what actions-as-cause we have made that result in our being angry, sad, and jealous. To find the seeds from actions done in the past, we need only to look at the fruits in the present moment.

The phrase "realms of being" in this verse again refers to the three realms of samsaric existence that we first discussed in Chapter Three. These are the realms of desire, form, and non-form. The realm of desire corresponds to the first stage of being. The realms of form and non-form are further divided into four levels each. The stages in the verse above refer to all nine levels of the three realms: the realm of desire, the four states of meditative concentration (*dhyana*) of the realm of form, and the four levels of the realm of non-form. The nine stages are:

1) The Realm of Desire (kamadhatu). Characteristic of this world is a lot of desire, running after things, and clinging. The Buddha described six destinations or modes of existence to which living beings migrate lifetime after lifetime: the world of the gods (*deva*); the world of the *ashuras*, beings who are talented and intelligent, yet angry and hostile; the world of human beings; the world of the hell realms; the world of the hungry ghosts (*preta*), those who are hungry for food, shelter, love, or something to believe in every day of their lives, yet who can never be satisfied; and the world of animals, those beings who live only by their instincts, who have no spiritual life, ideals, or compassion. These six kinds of beings—gods, ashuras, humans, hungry ghosts, hell beings, and animals—are all found in the realm of desire.

2) Brahma Heaven. This is the first level of the realm of form (rupadhatu). It is called the heavenly realm of the first dhyana. Beings of this world have bodies different from one another, but they think very much in the same way.

3) The Pure Heaven of Great Light. This is the second level of the realm of form, the heavenly realm of the second dhyana. There is much light in this world. The bodies of the beings of this world here are alike but their way of thinking differs.

4) The Everywhere-Pure Heaven. This is the third level of the realm of form. It is called the heavenly realm of the third dhyana and it is very peaceful and pure. The beings who live here are exactly alike in body and mind.

5) The Heaven of No-Perception. This is the fourth level of the realm of form and the highest of the four dhyana realms. At this level, beings do not have perception accompanied by ideation.

6) The Realm of Limitless Space is the first level of the realm of non-form (arupadhatu).

7) The Realm of Limitless Consciousness is the second level of the realm of non-form.

8) The Realm of No Object is the third level of the realm of non-form.

9) The Realm of No Perception and No Non-Perception is the fourth and final level of the realm of non-form.

The three realms and the nine stages are present because of the cooperation of the consciousnesses of many people. For example, the community of Plum Village in the southwest of France, where I live, is the collective manifestation of the consciousnesses of the teacher, the disciples, the friends on the path, and the community of practice that has been established there. We all have the motivation to study and practice, and so we have created Plum Village to do so. Whether you live in the desire realm, the form realm, or the formless realm, that realm is the creation of the collective consciousness of all those who inhabit it.

When we are in the desire realm, that is not only a manifestation of our individual consciousness but also of the collective consciousness. Western society is a consumer society, but the practitioners at Plum Village are not participating in the consumer society at the level of most people in Paris or

Bordeaux. Yet we are still living in the desire realm, which is a manifestation of collective consciousness. Television advertising is cleverly designed to water the seeds of desire in us. In Plum Village we do not watch television, so our seeds of desire cannot be watered through that particular medium. This is an individual manifestation within the collective manifestation of the consumer society.

The maturation of store consciousness also follows the Law of Affinity, the attraction of like to like. We do this, and we do not do that. The reasons why we do one thing and not another are already determined in the "maturation-as-cause" that leads to the "maturation-as-fruit." One example of maturation-as-fruit is the presence of Plum Village and the community of practice there. Maturation-as-cause are the seeds we sowed in the past that have drawn us to that place. This is called "the force of action," in this case a wholesome action. If we had the seeds of drug addiction, we would not go there. But because we have watered the seeds of Buddhadharma in ourselves, we are drawn to it. The community of Plum Village is, in this sense, predetermined. Wholesome seeds have already been sown and watered in our store consciousness, and now they are sprouting. They give us the energy to come and participate in a community of practice.

One day, sitting in the Jeta Grove, the Buddha observed, "Monks, do you see that the monks who enjoy Dharma discussion are sitting close to the Venerable Shariputra and those who are interested in the precepts are sitting with the Venerable Upali? The monks who like to give Dharma talks are gathered around the Venerable Purna. Shariputra is very good in Dharma discussion, Upali is an expert in the precepts, and Purna gives excellent Dharma talks." This is an example of the Law of Affinity. Our aspirations, our needs, and the energy of our actions determine whether we participate in one realm or stage of being or another. When we find a friend we enjoy spending time with, there is the law of attraction of like to like. We feel we have an affinity with this person, and this information is recorded as a seed in our consciousness. When the seed of affinity ripens, we find ourselves drawn to a particular person or situation.

Plum Village is a small area and Europe is a large area. We belong to the large area, and we come and participate in the small area. Yet when we are in Plum Village, we are also in Europe. Similarly, when we participate in one of the nine stages of being, it does not mean that we are not also participating in the other eight stages, only that our participation in them is more diluted. Our participation in the stage to which we are drawn due to the Law of Affinity is always more concentrated—but we are still participating in the other stages. All nine stages exist within us. When one manifests, the others are less distinct but they are nonetheless present.

Maturation is the ripe fruit of our consciousness. At the time of maturation, our consciousness seeks to dwell in the stage that is closest to the sum of our actions. If we have an action in our store consciousness associated with addiction to cocaine, the force of attraction of like to like naturally leads us to associate with others who like drugs. Maturation of the fruit in consciousness leads us toward one of the realms in a very deep way.

Let us look deeply into this book. This book is a manifestation of our collective consciousness, because each of you has planted in your store consciousness the seed of the practice. Perhaps you have read another book or have heard about mindfulness practice or Buddhist psychology, and you have the desire to cultivate more insight into the art of healing and transformation. This may have happened some time ago. Now conditions are sufficient for me to offer this book and for you to read it. The participation of each of us depends on the actions we have performed in the past. Why aren't others reading about these Fifty Verses? Because they do not share the same interest. But something has determined that we come together in this way. It has been recorded in our store consciousness, collective and individual. This is the Law of Affinity, or participation.

Each of us has the capacity within ourselves to exist in all six realms of being—the realms of the gods, the ashuras (angry gods or demons), humans, hungry ghosts, the hell realms, and the realm of the animals. We all have been in hell. Hell is not very far away. Hell is right here. In the Buddhist tradition, we believe that there are beings called hungry ghosts. A hungry ghost has a very big belly and a throat as small as a needle. Hungry ghosts can never satisfy their hunger. Every year in Buddhist countries on the full-moon day of the eighth lunar month, we make offerings to our ancestors. Ancestors are not hungry ghosts. They have children and a place to come home to. But we know that there are many hungry ghosts wandering around who don't have a home. That is why we also make offerings of rice cakes, water, and so on to the hungry ghosts. We recite mantras to bring the size of the hungry ghosts' throats back to normal. Then we read the Heart Sutra and invite the hungry ghosts to come and eat.[10] And we pray to Amitabha Buddha to bring all the hungry ghosts to the Pure Land.[11]

Hungry ghosts are not just beings of traditional Buddhist belief. Our society creates thousands of hungry ghosts every day. Looking deeply, we see that they are everywhere around us. These are people without roots. In their family, their parents did not demonstrate that happiness is possible. They did not feel understood or accepted by their church or community. So they have rejected everything. They don't believe in family, society, or religion. They don't believe in their own traditions. But they are still looking for something good, beautiful, and true to believe in; they are hungry for understanding and love.

From time to time hungry ghosts come to a practice center like Plum Village. We can recognize them easily. Even if you offer them understanding and love, they are skeptical. To help a hungry ghost, you have to be patient. You have to earn their trust first. But because their throats are so tiny—they are suspicious of everything, not ready to believe in anything—even if you have love to offer they cannot accept it. And, because of the Law of Affinity, hungry ghosts also like to come together with other hungry ghosts. If we water the seed of the hungry ghost in ourself, we will become a hungry ghost. Then we will look for other hungry ghosts to spend time with and we will form a society of hungry ghosts.

Whether we go in the direction of gods, humans, ashuras, hungry ghosts, hell, or animals is already established within our store consciousness. Karma means action, the actions of body, speech, and mind. Every act, word, and thought in our daily life has the power to bring forth a fruit. When our actions of body, speech, and mind come together and have time

10 The Heart Sutra (Prajñaparamita-hridaya-sutra) is one of the most popular and important texts of Mahayana Buddhism. It is said to contain the "heart," or essence, of the Mahayana Prajñaparamita teachings (see note 14). See Thich Nhat Hanh, *The Heart of Understanding: Commentaries on the Prajñaparamita Heart Sutra* (Berkeley, CA: Parallax Press, 1988).

11 The Pure Land school of Mahayana Buddhism emphasizes faith in the power and compassion of Amitabha, the Buddha of the Western Paradise, to bring his devotees to be reborn in his Pure Land. For more on the Pure Land, see *Finding Our True Home* (Berkeley, CA: Parallax Press, 2004).

to ripen, store consciousness undergoes maturation and brings forth another stage of being. After years of living, performing actions of body, speech, and mind, the participation of our individual store consciousness in the collective consciousness is manifested in the realm of being that we go to.

Suppose someone is caught in a cycle of drug-taking. He is attracted to that environment no matter where he goes. This is the manifestation of his store consciousness. The maturation of his past actions leads him in that direction. The participation of his store consciousness in that realm of being is the fruit of his way of life. But if he meets someone who is capable of loving and helping him, the positive seeds in him are watered and he might get some insight. With the help of the other person, he might be able to disassociate himself from the unwholesome environment. Slowly, the maturation of other seeds will help him move toward and participate in another realm of being.

The seeds in us lead us to share the life of others who are like us—whether that life is wholesome or unwholesome. Transformation, however, is possible. First, we have to determine in what direction we wish to go. Second, we have to wish to embark on a journey of transformation and healing. Third, we discover that there is a path that we can embrace and we look for a way to practice with others who also want to live more mindfully. Then we discover that we share the same karma, the karma of practicing healing and transforming. Those who are interested only in eating, sleeping, and having sex will come together in the realm of desire. Those who are concerned about the suffering people in the world will find ways to come together in order to serve. This is the Law of Affinity.

Emancipation—participation in the realm of joy and peace—is a matter of touching and transforming the seeds, of helping the positive seeds grow. We don't need to die in order to be reborn and have a new being. A few weeks or months of practicing in order to transform can help ripen the wholesome seeds in us and bring about a new life here and now. Taking care of our seeds, planting and watering the good ones, not helping negative ones to manifest, we are going on the path of maturation. I have seen people who, after only three or four days of practice, came out as new beings. They could go home and reconcile with members of their family and restore the happiness they deserve. The seeds of beginning anew, looking deeply, transformation, and healing in them were well taken care of, and maturation could take place quickly. We too are capable of producing a new being from the seeds in our consciousness, of living in a more positive and happy way. There is no reason to think we cannot.

IO

The Five Universals

Unobstructed and indeterminate,
store consciousness is continuously flowing and changing.
At the same time, it is endowed
with all five universal mental formations.

THIS VERSE describes qualities of the store consciousness that differentiate it from the other consciousnesses. "Unobstructed" means exposed to the light, not hidden. Store consciousness is unobstructed because it has the capacity of attaining absolute clarity. It is also indeterminate, meaning that store consciousness itself is neither wholesome nor unwholesome, though it contains all the seeds, both wholesome and unwholesome.

All phenomena are of one of three natures: wholesome (*kushala*), unwholesome (*akushala*), and indeterminate (*aniyata*). Our every action, word, and thought belongs to one of these natures. Wholesome means useful to ourselves and others. Unwholesome means harmful to ourselves and others. Indeterminate means that an action, word, or thought is neither inherently wholesome nor unwholesome. It can be either, depending on the circumstances. Whether it is harmful or helpful depends on our way of living.

Store consciousness operates continuously, day and night, without stopping. The six sense consciousnesses of eye, ear, nose, tongue, body, and mind are sometimes active and sometimes at rest. Eye consciousness, for example, operates during the day but not when we are asleep, because our eyes are closed and do not perceive any object. Only through contact with its object does a sense base give rise to a sense consciousness. If we are asleep and not dreaming, mind consciousness stops also. The seventh consciousness, manas, however, which is closely affiliated with the store consciousness and acts as the support of mind consciousness, does not stop. Like store consciousness, manas never ceases in its activity. We will learn more about manas in the next section of this book.

Even though store consciousness never ceases, this doesn't mean that it is always the same. It is continuously flowing and changing, like a river. A river is always the same river, but the water in it is always changing. Store consciousness is the same. It is the river, and the seeds it contains are like the water that is changing all the time.

The term "mental formations" is a very important term in Buddhism, and it is one we will encounter throughout this book. A mental formation is the result of the manifestation of a seed in our store consciousness. The Manifestation Only school divides mental formations into fifty-one categories, which we will discuss in detail later in the Fifty Verses. To understand this verse, we need to know that there are five universal mental formations: contact (*sparsha*), attention (*manaskara*), feeling (*vedana*), perception, or conceptualization (*samjña*), and volition (*chetana*). These five mental formations are "associated" (*samprayukta*), which means they are engaged with each other. They are called universal because they are active in all eight consciousnesses.

The five universal mental formations (*sarvatraga*) function with the eighth consciousness in terms of receiving, accepting, holding, maintaining, preserving, and storing the seeds, which are the functions of store consciousness. Store consciousness operates in the form of these five universal mental formations. However, the five universals are different in each of the other consciousnesses, because the mode of perception (*pramana*, "way of measuring") of store consciousness is different from the mode of perception of other consciousnesses.

To understand how the consciousnesses operate, we have to consider the nature, mode, and object of perception of each. In Chapter Eight we discussed the three fields of perception—the realms of things-in-themselves, the realm of representations, and the realm of mere images. The mode of perception that leads to the realm of things-in-themselves is direct (*pratyaksha pramana*). A direct perception does not involve thought or imagination; it is not the result of comparison or reasoning. In the store consciousness, the mode of perception is always direct. When we see a fire, we know that it is a fire. This is a direct perception.

But suppose we see smoke rising from behind a wall and from that we surmise that there must be a fire there. This is a deduced perception, perception by inference (*anumana pramana*), and it may be either correct or incorrect. If what we thought was smoke from a fire is actually mist, for example, and if on seeing the mist we say there is a fire, that is an erroneous perception (*abhava pramana*). The Buddha warned that most of our perceptions are false. When we look at a beautiful sunset, we believe that we perceive the sun of the present moment. But scientists tell us that the sun we are seeing is actually an image of the sun of eight minutes earlier. We go through our lives with many erroneous perceptions, yet we are certain they are all correct. False perception is the source of so much suffering.

The store consciousness does not engage in thinking, comparing, or imagining. Its mode of perception is always direct. Therefore, the mode of the five universal mental formations as they function with the store consciousness is also always direct. In the eighth consciousness, contact is direct; mental attention is direct; and feeling, perception, and volition are also direct. But this is not necessarily true of the functioning of these five mental formations in the other consciousnesses, because the nature and qualities of the other consciousnesses differ.

The five universals are not separate from the mind—the mind is the content of the mind. The nature of the store consciousness is also the nature of these five universal mental formations. Our store consciousness and the five universal mental formations of that consciousness—both subject and object—are all unobstructed and indeterminate, changing and constantly flowing. Every seed, every object, and every perception are like drops of water in the river of the store consciousness, and they take on the nature of that consciousness.

The qualities of the store consciousness that make it unique are also the same qualities that allow for transformation of the seeds it contains. Because store consciousness is unobstructed and indeterminate, because its nature is neutral, and because it is always flowing and changing, it can be transformed. Every day is an opportunity for transformation. When we transform the seeds in our store consciousness, that is transformation at the base.

II

The Three Dharma Seals

Although impermanent and without a separate self,
store consciousness contains all phenomena in the cosmos,
both conditioned and unconditioned,
in the form of seeds.

PHENOMENA (DHARMAS) can be categorized into two groups: those that have leaks (*ashrava*), and those that are without leaks (*anashrava*). "With leaks" means that there is still something dripping out, like water from a cracked earthenware jar. It means that the action or experience does not have the nature of true insight and liberation—there is still the possibility of falling down and turning back, of the fruits of our actions (karmaphala) creating more seeds of delusion in our consciousness. "Without leaks" means that an action or experience has no more seepage, and it will produce no unwholesome karmic fruit.

Suppose we have a feeling of joy. This feeling may be with or without leaks. If the experience is unstable because our understanding is superficial, our feeling of joy might be leaky. When we discover the truth of something and have understanding and insight, that feeling of joy is pure, and we say it is without leaks. We will not fall back into our former state of mind. States of being that are with and without leaks are not necessarily opposites. If we do not see the essence of something, our seeing still has leaks.

Phenomena "with leaks" belong to the world of birth, death, and suffering, the world of samsara. This is the historical dimension. Phenomena without leaks belong to the world of no birth and no death, nirvana, the ultimate dimension. It is important to remember that the historical and ultimate dimensions are part of the same reality. A wave has two dimensions—the historical and the ultimate. Dwelling only in the historical dimension—the wave—is living in samsara. But if we can realize that the true nature of a wave is water, our fear will dissolve and we will be in the ultimate dimension, nirvana. The wave does not have to become water—it already is water. The historical dimension does not exist separately from the ultimate dimension.

In the historical dimension, phenomena seem to have leaks, but as soon as we touch them deeply with our insight, we move into the ultimate dimension and there are no longer any leaks. Whether we are in the historical or ultimate dimension has everything to do with our perceptions. Usually, we have many opposite notions about phenomena: birth and death, superiority and inferiority, high and low, beautiful and ugly. All these perceptions can be described as samsara, and they make us suffer. If we remember that the wave is, at the same time, water, we will transcend all dualistic concepts and fear and suffering will cease. The things that we perceive as being born and dying, enduring and being cut off, coming and going, or many and one in the historical dimension are no longer seen as being born and dying, enduring and being cut off, coming and going, or existing and ceasing to exist in the ultimate dimension. These phenomena have all been purified. They are without leaks.

Whether our actions are with or without leaks also depends on our way of looking. We can help a hungry child, save the life of a caterpillar, or stop someone from harming themselves or others, yet these beneficial actions could have leaks even though they bring about joy and a good result. If we do things in such a way that we are not pulled along by dualistic ideas of space, time, self, other, and so on, our actions are pure.

We can easily see whether an action is pure or not. Suppose someone visits an orphanage and they are asked to sign their name in a book and record the donation they have given. The way that person signs their name will reveal whether their donation is pure. If they donate a hundred dollars because they think that it won't look good to give too little, their act of generosity has leaks. If the visitor doesn't view the logbook as a record of how much money others have given and they give a hundred dollars without thinking about whether or not it will look good in comparison, their action is pure. When they give, they do not say to themselves, "I am helping an orphan, someone in difficulty," which is a way of seeing themselves as separate from those whom they help. Instead, their generosity comes out of their realization that life is impermanent, and they act purely out of love.

Actions with leaks lie within the realm of birth and death, the historical dimension. They can help relieve suffering, or they can cause further suffering. But purified acts can bring us to liberation and nonattachment and help us to not fall back into lower realms of existence.[12] The two kinds of action cannot be compared. Purified action does not calculate the amount of work required, or the glory and benefits that may accrue. It arises naturally from insight and freedom. For this reason, the happiness brought about by a purified action is much greater, because it is liberated and not based on external signs. "With leaks" means to be attached to the cycle of birth and death. "Without leaks" means liberation.

A flower, our anger, space, and time are all types of phenomena, or dharmas. There are conditioned (*samskrita*) and unconditioned (*asamskrita*) dharmas. The deluded mind can touch only conditioned phenomena, which constantly undergo changes, including birth and death. In nirvana, there are only unconditioned phenomena that do not undergo birth and death. But if we look deeply, we find that the true nature of *all* phenomena is nirvana. Everything has been "nirvanized" since the non-beginning. The Diamond Sutra and other sutras from the Mahayana Prajñaparamita literature help us touch deeply the no-birth, no-death nature of all phenomena.[13] The cosmos (*dharmadhatu*), the realm where all phenomena manifest, includes everything.

A flower is a conditioned phenomenon. A flower needs a certain combination of conditions working together—a seed, soil, sunshine, clouds,

12 The six modes, or destinations, into which living beings migrate as a result of their actions (karma) are divided into the three higher realms of devas (gods), ashuras (powerful, angry gods who are hostile to the devas), and human beings; and the three lower realms of the hungry ghosts, the hells, and the animals. While all six modes are still part of samsaric existence, beings of the three higher realms, especially human beings, are able to transform their consciousness and create conditions for a favorable rebirth, while beings of the three lower realms cannot easily find release from the cycle of samsara.

13 See Thich Nhat Hanh, *The Diamond That Cuts through Illusion: Commentaries on the Prajñaparamita Diamond Sutra* (Berkeley, CA: Parallax Press, 1992). The Prajñaparamita ("Perfection of Wisdom") sutras are a collection of about forty texts composed around the first century C.E. which represent a fundamental source of Mahayana teachings on the realization of *prajña* (wisdom). This body of literature was very influential in the development of the thought and practice of later major Buddhist schools, including the Ch'an (Zen) school.

rain, earth, a gardener, and our own consciousness—in order to come to be. It is born and it will die. When we say that something is conditioned, we mean that it has to inter-be with everything else. It cannot exist independently. When we look deeply into the heart of a flower, we see that the flower cannot be by itself alone. Because it does not have any independent, permanent existence, we say that it is empty of a separate self. Because the flower is of the nature of nonself and impermanence, this means that it is at the same time full of everything in the cosmos. If you touch a flower deeply, you touch the whole cosmos.

Some schools of Buddhism say that space is an unconditioned dharma. For me, space is a conditioned dharma. Space is made of time and, without consciousness, space is not possible. Our store consciousness is also like this. Like everything else, it is impermanent and without a separate self. All mental formations that arise from our store consciousness are also impermanent and without a separate self. This consciousness is made of other consciousnesses, and other consciousnesses are made of this consciousness. We can see interbeing in the very heart of our own store consciousness.

When we look into a flower, we can see that it contains the whole cosmos—sunshine, clouds, time, space, and even our consciousness. Store consciousness is also like this: it contains all phenomena, conditioned and unconditioned. Most things manifest themselves as formations, based on conditions. But some things do not rely on anything to manifest. These unconditioned dharmas are nirvana, the ultimate dimension. Within our store consciousness are the seeds of the unconditioned. Nirvana is already within us.

Impermanence, nonself, and nirvana are called the Three Dharma Seals. The Buddha speaks of them as the keys to open the door of reality, to touch every phenomenon deeply. Mindfulness is the energy we can use to be in touch with phenomena in the realm of form. When we are in touch with our liver, for example, our liver feels this and is very happy to receive our attention. If we use our mindfulness to touch it deeply enough, we see its impermanent nature. It is constantly changing. Even if our liver was healthy three months ago, that does not guarantee it will be in good health forever, especially if we do not look after it and take care of it. At the same time, we see the nonself, interdependent nature of our liver. The well-being of our liver depends on many other elements, like the health of our entire digestive system, the things we eat and drink, even hereditary factors.

When we look deeply into the impermanent and nonself nature of our liver, we begin to understand the difficulties it has. We feel love and wish to care for it, and our way of acting can transform the state of our liver. The same applies to our lungs, our heart, and every other part of our body. We stop smoking, eating, and drinking in ways that cause our liver to wear out, our lungs to malfunction, or the flow of blood to and from our heart to be constricted. When we use the Three Dharma Seals given to us by the Buddha as a key to open the door to the reality of our bodies, we come to understand them deeply. Only when we understand them deeply will we look after them carefully.

In the same way, we can use these three keys to open the door of reality of all phenomena. The first two keys, impermanence and nonself, help us discover the historical dimension of phenomena. When we are deeply in touch with the world around us, we are in the sphere of the third key, nirvana, and we feel at ease and without fear. When we go even deeper, we can touch the ultimate dimension of our body, our feelings, our perceptions, and our mental formations. Through mindfulness, we can touch our sadness, anger, or anxiety. This is the main pillar of meditation practice taught by the Buddha. The study of consciousness can help us even more.

Impermanence and nonself are in essence the same. They both mean the absence of a separate, fixed self. It is called impermanence when looked at from the angle of time, and nonself when looked at from the angle of space. Our store consciousness is impermanent and without a separate self, and it contains within itself all dharmas, both conditioned and unconditioned, in the cosmos (dharmadhatu), just as a flower contains within itself the entire cosmos. The realm of things-in-themselves can be found in a flower and in our store consciousness. The realms of representations and of mere images are also found in a flower and within our store consciousness.

Do you have your own separate store consciousness? The answer can be yes, as long as you know that the individual is made of the collective. Where in your body is your store consciousness? It is present in every cell of your body. You can touch the whole of store consciousness in any cell of your body. Cloning is possible because each cell of our body contains within itself the potential to recreate our entire body. Healing techniques like acupuncture and reflexology also demonstrate that you can touch the whole body by touching just one part of it.

Our store consciousness cannot exist by itself alone. It has to inter-be with other consciousnesses. The one contains and is made of the all, and the all contains and is made of the one. The collective is made of the individual, and the individual is made of the collective. This insight helps us remove the notions of "individual" and "collective." Looking deeply into the nature of store consciousness, we can see that its true nature is neither individual nor collective, but simultaneously individual and collective. After removing notions of complete individuality and complete collectivity, we can begin to see the real nondual nature of store consciousness.

12

Seeds and Formations

Seeds can produce seeds.
Seeds can produce formations.
Formations can produce seeds.
Formations can produce formations.

PHENOMENA (DHARMAS) may be present in the form of seeds or formations. "Seed" means something that has the capacity of manifesting. "Formation" means what has been manifested. This verse describes the connection between seeds and formations. When we don't feel angry, the seed of anger has not manifested, though it is still present in our store consciousness. When someone says something unpleasant or hurtful to us, he waters the seed of anger in us. The seed manifests itself in our mind consciousness and becomes a mental formation.

A seed can influence other seeds within the store consciousness without the intervention of mind consciousness. Suppose we have a seed of despair in us and it is watered many times until it grows and becomes very strong. When it has been watered enough it will manifest in our mind consciousness. When a seed manifests in our mind consciousness it has become a formation, and in the process it has been strengthened. Anything that has a chance to manifest is strengthened. A seed, once manifested, can then produce other seeds of the same nature in our store consciousness. When anger is manifested as a formation in our mind consciousness, if the energy of mindfulness does not take care of it, the formation that is manifested will help to strengthen the seed of anger in our store consciousness.

Seeds never remain the same forever. They always undergo transformation and change. Seeds within our store consciousness undergo birth and death in every moment. The formations that manifest from these seeds also undergo birth and death in every moment. And our body as a formation undergoes birth and death in every moment, also. Birth and death take place in every moment in our consciousness and in every cell of our body. Each seed and each formation undergo the process of birth and death in the context of conditions. A seed doesn't necessarily disappear when the formation is manifested. Seeds and formations inter-are.

The seed of anger in our store consciousness, when manifested into the energy of anger in our mind consciousness as a formation, continues to exist as a seed at the same time. After manifesting for some time in the upper level of our consciousness, our anger will return to the root and the seed will become a little bit stronger. If we allow any seed to have occasion to manifest as a formation, that seed grows bigger and stronger. If we know how to touch the seeds of compassion, forgiveness, and joy in us and have them manifest several times a day, those seeds will become more and more important in our store consciousness. If we touch the seeds of fear, anger, and pain in ourselves and allow people around us to touch them also, we are helping those seeds grow stronger all the time.

When we are angry, we suffer. We believe that if we express our anger we will get some relief. Some therapists advise their clients to "get in touch with your anger" or "get it out of your system." There is a therapeutic practice to have a client go into a room and beat on a pillow. The theory is that this is a safe way for someone to express anger instead of actually beating up another person. But expressing anger may multiply it manyfold. When we hit a pillow, we are rehearsing our anger and helping the seed of anger in us grow. I do not think this is a wise practice but in fact a dangerous practice, because while you are beating the pillow and expressing the anger that has already manifested, you are at the same time strengthening the seed of anger at the base.

It is not that we should repress our anger. It is important to learn to embrace our anger, to recognize it and allow it to be. Then we can touch it with our mindfulness in order to transform it. When we beat a pillow, we are not really touching our anger mindfully. We are allowing ourselves to be overwhelmed by our anger. In fact, we are not even in touch with the pillow. If we were really in touch with the pillow, we would know that it is only a pillow and we wouldn't want to pound it like that. The practice of mindfulness is crucial for recognizing our anger, allowing it to be, touching it, and transforming it. Every time a negative formation is recognized, it loses some of its strength. That is why mindful breathing and walking, and using our mindfulness to embrace and recognize mental formations as they manifest is so important. We need the energy of mindfulness to take care of our anger in a safe way.

We should strive to learn to identify all the positive and negative seeds in us. Then we can refrain from watering the negative seeds, and use every opportunity to water the positive seeds. This is called "selective watering." It is very important to practice this in our relationships. Try to understand the situation of the person you love and refrain from watering his or her negative seeds. Practice watering only the positive seeds. Tell your partner, "Darling, if you really love me, do not touch the negative seeds in me too often." The two of you should sign an agreement, a peace treaty, agreeing to take care of each other's seeds. Watering only positive seeds will bring about positive change in the other person, and these positive changes will come back to you in the form of greater joy, peace, and happiness.

13

Indra's Net

Seeds and formations
both have the nature of interbeing and interpenetration.
The one is produced by the all.
The all is dependent on the one.

THE THIRTEENTH AND FOURTEENTH verses represent the contribution of the Avatamsaka Sutra to the Manifestation Only teachings. The brothers Asanga and Vasubandhu began the Vijñanavada school in the fourth century.[14] At that time, the teachings of the Avatamsaka school were not included in the system of Buddhist psychology, which was based on the Abhidharma of Original Buddhism. In the seventh century, Master Xuanzang brought the Vijñanavada teachings to China, but the Avatamsaka teachings had still not been incorporated into them. The third patriarch of the Avatamsaka school in China, Fazang (643–712), was the first to bring these important Mahayana teachings into this system of Buddhist psychology in his book, *Notes on the Mystical in the Avatamsaka Sutra.*

In the thirteenth verse we encounter the teaching of interbeing and interpenetration as presented in the Avatamsaka Sutra. The Avatamsaka Sutra is the source of the image of Indra's net which is part of the god Indra's heaven.[15] Indra's net is a vast, cosmic lattice that contains precious jewels wherever the threads cross. There are millions of jewels strung together to make the net, and each jewel has many facets. When you look at any facet of any one jewel, you can see all the other jewels reflected in it. In the world

14 See Afterword.
15 Indra, a deity from Hindu mythology, is one of many such figures that were retained in Indian Buddhist teachings. The Tushita heaven of Buddhism corresponds to Indra heaven of Hinduism.

of the Avatamsaka, in Indra's net, the one is present in the all, and the all is present in the one. This wonderful image was used in Buddhism to illustrate the principle of interdependence and interpenetration.

In our ordinary discriminatory world, we see a teapot as a single, independent object. But if we look deeply enough into the teapot, we will see that it contains many phenomena—earth, water, fire, air, space, and time—and we will realize that in fact the entire universe has come together to make this teapot. That is the interdependent nature of the teapot. A flower is made up of many non-flower elements, such as clouds, soil, and sunshine. Without clouds and earth, there could be no flower. This is interbeing. The one is the result of the all. What makes the all possible is the one.

We can see the nature of interbeing and interpenetration in every seed and formation. Interpenetration means that the all is in one. The flower cannot exist by itself alone. It has to inter-be with everything else. All phenomena are like that. The Buddha said, "This is, because that is." This is a simple but profound teaching. It means that everything is related to everything else. Everything enters into and is entered into by everything else. The sunshine penetrates the vegetation, the vegetation penetrates animals, and we interpenetrate each other. In the one, we see the all. In the all, we see the one. In the one you touch the all, and in the all you touch the one. This is the teaching of the Avatamsaka Sutra, the deepest teaching of interconnectedness in Buddhism.

The British nuclear physicist David Bohm proposed the terms "explicate order" and "implicate order" to describe what Buddhist teachings call ordinary and ultimate reality. In the explicate order, everything exists outside of everything else. The elephant exists outside of the rose, the table exists outside of the forest, you exist outside of me, and so on. The explicate order is what we see when we don't look into things very deeply. But, as Bohm discovered, when we look more deeply into the nature of each so-called elementary particle, we see that one particle is made of all other particles. The notions we use in our daily life can no longer be applied in the domain of the infinitely small. In one particle you can identify the existence of all other particles. Looking deeply into the nature of a particle reveals to us the implicate order, where everything is inside of everything else.

The implicate order is the same as the ultimate dimension, and the explicate order is equivalent to the historical dimension. In the historical dimension there are notions of birth and death, beginning and end, this and that, being and nonbeing. But in the ultimate dimension there is no birth and death, beginning and ending, being and nonbeing. The ultimate dimension cannot be described in words and notions that by their very nature serve to cut reality up into separate pieces.

Of course, to communicate with others, to study Buddhism, we have to use words, ideas, and notions. In the end, however, we have to remove all of these notions in order for true understanding to be possible. Words like "same" and "different," "collective" and "individual" are just steps on a ladder. We have to go up to the next step and not be caught by these ideas. As long as we are caught in notions, ideas, and words, we cannot arrive at true understanding and we will not reach the ultimate dimension.

Using the teaching of interpenetration found in the Avatamsaka Sutra, we can unlock the door of reality and get rid of our notions concerning the world. The concepts we use to frame reality will have to disintegrate. We know that we have lungs for breathing in and out. But when we look more deeply, we can see that the mountains and forests are also our lungs. Without them, we could not breathe in and out either. We have hearts that function well, and we know that we could not survive unless our hearts were there, pumping. But looking more deeply, we can see that the sun is our second heart. If that sun were to cease to operate, we would die right away, just the same as if the heart in our own body were to stop functioning. We see that our body is the body of the cosmos, and that the cosmos is our own body.

This insight is only possible when we see through notions of inside and outside, self and other. When we look through the eyes of the Avatamsaka Sutra, we see that the cosmos and all the phenomena in it are part of Indra's net. We realize that concepts such as one and many, coming and going, collective and individual, above and below, even being and nonbeing, cannot be applied to ultimate reality.

14

True and Not True

Store consciousness is neither the same nor different,
individual nor collective.
Same and different inter-are.
Collective and individual give rise to each other.

ARE MY STORE CONSCIOUSNESS and your store consciousness one or two? To say they are two is wrong, and to say that they are one is also wrong. You and I are not one, and we are also not two. One is an idea; two is also an idea. Neither idea accords exactly with reality. My store consciousness is made of yours, just as your store consciousness is made of mine. We cannot say whether they are the same or different, whether there is one store consciousness or many. Same and different inter-are. Same is made of different, and different is made of same. Notions of same and different, one and many, are pairs of opposites, and the truth always transcends opposites. The only way to remove our suffering and delusions is to change our dualistic way of thinking and transcend notions.

Every phenomenon has both a collective and an individual nature. Just as the one and the many have to work together to produce something, so the individual and the collective depend on each other to develop and transform. We have to go beyond such ideas as same and different, individual and collective. This is the teaching of the Three Shastras school, whose proponents studied and expanded upon the teachings of the Middle Way based on three *shastras* (commentaries): the Madhyamika-shastra by Nagarjuna, the Shastra in One Hundred Verses by Nagarjuna, and the Twelve Doors' Shastra by Deva. The Middle Way is the way that is not caught in concepts. The Manifestation Only teachings contain the flavor of both the Avatamsaka Sutra and these Three Shastras teachings.

According to Nagarjuna, we have to go beyond ideas of birth and death, one and many, coming and going, permanence and annihilation. Nagarjuna's refutation of these dualistic concepts is called the "Eight Negations." Birth is an idea that means something arises from nothing. If we observe deeply, we see that things are not like that. Something cannot arise from nothing. We already existed before our birth, although in a different form. Clouds are the past life of rain. Rain is a continuation of the clouds. When energy becomes matter, that is just a continuation. It is not that matter has been produced wholesale out of nothingness. The laws of physics and the teachings of Buddhism agree that something cannot be produced from nothing.

In the same way, something cannot become nothing; it cannot completely disappear and cease to exist. When we burn a piece of paper, the paper does not cease to exist; it becomes heat, ashes, and smoke. Heat penetrates the cosmos. Smoke and other gases rise into the air and form clouds, which give rise to rain. Ashes fall down to the earth and nurture the soil. Rain and soil are two of the conditions necessary for trees to grow. Later, the tree may become a piece of paper again. Looking in this way, we can see that even a piece of paper transcends birth and death.

The ideas of coming and going are also not true. We say, I came from that place and I am going to this place. Or we say: Before I was born I was in another place and after I die I will be someplace else. But we know from the teachings of interpenetration and interbeing that "here" and "there" are merely concepts, and that every place can be found in every other place. There is really nowhere to go to or come from in the ultimate dimension.

The idea of permanence means that something goes on existing as it is forever, that it never undergoes any change or transformation. This too is an incorrect idea. Everything is of the nature to change. The opposite idea, annihilation, means that when we die, our body and our consciousness cease to exist. We have already seen how something cannot become nothing. Our body and consciousness simply change form.

Our mind is like a sword. It cuts reality into pieces, separate from each other. But reality cannot be grasped by our discursive mind—the mind of imagination, discrimination, and discussion. We have to learn how to touch reality without using our usual patterns of thinking. If we practice looking into the nature of interbeing of things, we can unlock the door of reality and let go of the notions of same and different, individual and collective. These are ideas that cannot be applied to ultimate reality.

The fourteenth verse helps us transcend the notions of same and different, collective and individual. These pairs of notions create each other, like left and right, above and below. Once we've used these notions to practice deep looking, we must let them go if we want to really understand. This verse can help us do that. If you believe that your store consciousness is the same as mine, you are caught in the notion of permanence. If you think that your store consciousness is not the same, you are caught in the other extreme. We have to let go of these notions to see the true nature of store consciousness, which is neither individual nor collective *and* both individual and collective.

If we are not able to transcend notions and concepts, we will get caught by the teaching or the concept. The Buddha said that his teaching is like a snake—it is dangerous. There is a sutra that describes how being caught in the teachings is exactly like being bitten by a snake that you are trying to catch.[16] In the sutra, the Buddha says that the best way to catch a snake is to use a forked stick to hold the head of the snake so you can grasp the snake behind its head so you cannot be harmed. If you try to grasp the snake with your hand alone, you will be bitten. Studying the teachings is the same. An intelligent person will not grasp onto ideas and notions and mistake them for reality.

16 See Thich Nhat Hanh, *Thundering Silence: Sutra on Knowing the Better Way to Catch a Snake* (Berkeley, CA: Parallax Press, 1993).

15

Great Mirror Wisdom

When delusion is overcome, understanding is there,
and store consciousness is no longer subject to afflictions.
Store consciousness becomes Great Mirror Wisdom,
reflecting the cosmos in all directions.
Its name is now Pure Consciousness.

WHEN, THANKS TO THE PRACTICE, darkness comes to an end, clarity arises and our store consciousness becomes pure. When delusion is transformed, understanding is there. Delusion, or ignorance, is the base for all our wrong perceptions, which create a lot of suffering. Through the practice of looking deeply into the nature of interbeing, delusion or ignorance can be transformed into *prajña*, wisdom or understanding.

Ignorance is one of the twelve links in the chain of Interdependent Co-Arising *(pratitya-samutpada)*.[17] Interdependent Co-Arising is a basic Buddhist teaching. It says that all psychological and physical phenomena (dharmas) that make up what we know as existence are interdependent and mutually condition each other. Each of the twelve links (*nidana*) in the chain of Interdependent Co-Arising conditions the next. Ignorance (*avidya*) conditions impulses (*samskara*). Impulses condition consciousness (*vijñana*). Consciousness conditions mind/body, also called name and form (*namarupa*). Mind/body conditions the six sense organs (*shadayatana*). The six sense organs condition contact (*sparsha*). Contact conditions feeling (*vedana*). Feeling conditions craving (*trishna*). Craving conditions grasping (*upadana*). Grasping conditions becoming (*bhava*). Becoming conditions

17 For an in-depth discussion of Interdependent Co-Arising, see Thich Nhat Hanh, *The Heart of the Buddha's Teaching*, Chapter 27.

birth (*jati*). And birth conditions old age and death (*jara-maranam*). Interdependent Co-Arising is the engine that drives the cycle of samsara. Ignorance, the first link, is the prime cause of suffering.

The Sanskrit term for ignorance is avidya, which means the absence of knowledge. This is the absence of understanding. Because of our ignorance or delusion, we plant and water many unwholesome seeds in our store consciousness. If we look deeply, we can get some insight and transform these seeds. As we continue to practice, our ignorance diminishes and our understanding increases. There is a point when ignorance is completely transformed and understanding becomes a reality. Sometimes wisdom, prajña, is called pure consciousness (*vimala vijñana*). When our store consciousness is completely purified, it is no longer able to be overcome by afflictions (*klesha*)—mental formations such as fear, anger, hatred, and discrimination. After transformation, our store consciousness is free. It is transformed into the Great Mirror Wisdom, able to reflect the world of suchness without distortion.

There is so much ignorance and delusion in our usual way of perceiving and experiencing things that our store consciousness cannot reveal itself to us as a part of the ultimate dimension. But in fact the essential nature of store consciousness has always been free of afflictions. Only by looking deeply with the insight of nonself and interbeing can delusion be transformed and insight reveal to us the nature of suchness that we already have within ourselves.

Some practitioners think that there is nothing left once ignorance has been destroyed. Once they reach that point, all they have to do is pass over to another world. But, according to the Buddha, "When ignorance is no longer there, wisdom arises." When you remove the darkness, the light is there, and with light there is awakening. At that moment, everything that belongs to store consciousness, individual and collective, is purified. When free of impurities (*amala vijñana*), store consciousness becomes a mirror reflecting every aspect of existence without distortion. Birth, death, and suffering transform into peace, joy, awakening, and liberation. This is the "Pure Consciousness" that allows us to recognize and enter the realm of suchness in this very life.

Like the earth, store consciousness has the task of holding seeds. We know that store consciousness is itself neutral by nature. Wholesome or unwholesome seeds in the store consciousness manifest depending on the activity of the other consciousnesses. When the sun is shining, the earth gets warm. When it rains, the earth becomes wet. The seeds in the earth are then able to germinate and the plants grow, making the earth green. During the dry season and in the winter when there is less sunshine, the earth may not be green. But even then we can't say that the earth is lifeless. It continues its wonderful work, silently.

The other seven consciousnesses are the gardeners that till the earth. We study and practice using our six senses. The seeds of perception are brought into our store consciousness, and store consciousness begins its silent work, like the earth. As gardeners, we turn the soil, sow seeds, water them, pull weeds, and add fertilizer. But we cannot do the work of the earth. Only the earth can hold the seeds and bring forth the fruits of our labor. What is most important is to have faith that the earth will germinate the seeds that have been sown.

Suppose, in our practice, our teacher invites us to look deeply at a particular object during meditation. We should not try to do this work only with our intellect. Our intellect, our mind consciousness, is just the gardener. It cannot do the work of the store consciousness. Instead we should plant the object of our meditation in our store consciousness like a seed, and water it every day. Then, as we go about our activities during the day, walking, standing, lying down, or sitting, we water that seed through the practice of mindfulness. If we water the seed every day, one day, when we least expect it, the flower of understanding will appear to us as an offering from our store consciousness. If we try to use our mind consciousness to make the seed grow, the seed will dry up. A gardener cannot do the work of the soil.

When I was a child, one morning I saw a beautiful leaf lying at the bottom of a rainwater cistern. I wanted to reach in and pick it up, but my arm was too short to reach all the way down. So I took a stick and churned the water, hoping the leaf would rise to the surface. I grew tired of waiting for it to come up, so I threw the stick aside and went off to play. About ten minutes later, I came back and saw the leaf floating on the surface. After I'd left, the water continued to turn and that continued movement brought the leaf to the surface.

Our store consciousness is like that. When it receives orders from our mind consciousness to do something, it works day and night. Many of us have had the experience of walking down the street and meeting someone we recognize but whose name we can't remember. All the way home we try to remember the person's name. We know his name, but trying so hard to remember gives us a headache. So we decide to forget it for a while, read a book, and then go to sleep. During the night, while we are asleep, our store consciousness continues its work. We spent several hours using our mind consciousness to try and recall the name, but now we've entrusted the work of finding it to our store consciousness. During sleep, our mind consciousness stops working on the problem, but the store consciousness continues its work. The next morning, while we are brushing our teeth, the name leaps into our mind. The practice of meditation is like this. We have to trust our store consciousness. It isn't the intellect that does all the work. When we know how our store consciousness works, we will succeed in our practice.

This verse is the last one about store consciousness before we go on to the section of the Fifty Verses that deals with the seventh consciousness, manas. Actually, we never leave store consciousness. Store consciousness is the base, and we will not be able to fully transform our consciousness unless we transform it at the base. We will find store consciousness in the verses about manas, in the subsequent verses about mind consciousness, the five sense consciousnesses, the practice, and the path. The teachings of interbeing and interpenetration show us that is not possible to cut reality into pieces. The one contains the all. We only need to look deeply in order to see this.

Part II

Manas

Verses Sixteen to Twenty-Two are about the seventh consciousness, manas. The relationship between manas and the store consciousness is very subtle. Manas arises from store consciousness, and takes a part of store consciousness to be the object of its love, the object of itself, and it holds onto it firmly. It regards this part of store consciousness as a separate entity, a "self," and grasps on to it firmly. Manas attaches to the store consciousness just like a small child who clings to her mother's skirt, not allowing her to walk naturally. In the same way, manas hinders the functioning of the store consciousness and gets in the way of transforming the seeds.

Just as the moon's gravitational pull on the Earth causes the tides, the grip of manas on the store consciousness is the energy that brings about the manifestation of seeds as mental formations in our mind consciousness. Our habit energies, delusions, and craving come together and create a tremendous source of energy that conditions our actions, speech, and thinking. This energy is called manas. The function of manas is grasping.

Like store consciousness, the nature of manas is continuous. It functions day and night without stopping. We have learned about the three modes of perception. The first is direct, the second is by inference or deduction, which may be either correct or incorrect, and the third is erroneous. The mode of perception of manas is always this third mode, false perception. Because the wrong perception of manas, especially its view of a "self," is the cause of so much suffering, it is important to understand the role of manas in creating and maintaining erroneous perceptions.

16

Seeds of Delusion

Seeds of delusion give rise
to the internal formations of craving and afflictions.
These forces animate our consciousness
as mind and body manifest themselves.

WE KNOW THAT our store consciousness manifests as the world, both the instrumental world (the environment) and the sentient world (ourselves and other living beings). Our body is a manifestation of our store consciousness. Mind/body, or "name and form" (*namarupa*), manifest through the store consciousness. When manas, the seventh consciousness, is involved, however, the seeds of delusion in our store consciousness are able to manifest as mental formations, and suffering is the result.

You will recall that one of the names given to store consciousness is "store for the attachment to a self." This has to do with manas. Manas is the energy of ignorance, thirst, and craving. It arises from the store consciousness and turns back to grasp a part of store consciousness. In Chapter Eight, we discussed the three aspects of perception. The part of store consciousness that manas tries to grasp is that of the subject that perceives (*darshana-bhaga*). At this point, manas and store consciousness overlap and, as a result of this overlapping, an object of the grasping of manas is produced.

Manas grasps on to the image that it has created and clings to it as its object. That portion of store consciousness that is grasped by manas loses its freedom. Our mind is enslaved when it is picked up and embraced as a "self" by manas. Manas holds on to the object of its attraction very tightly, as if to say, "You are mine." It is a kind of love affair. In fact, manas is described as "love of self." It is really attachment to self. Manas is "the lover," store consciousness is the beloved, the nature of their love is attachment—and suffering is the result.

Based on manas, the sixth consciousness, mind consciousness, is brought about. The mind consciousness can function independently or in conjunction with the first five sense consciousnesses of eyes, ears, nose, tongue, and body. Manas also serves as our "survival instinct." If while sleeping soundly we hear a sudden noise and wake up, that is the functioning of manas. If someone throws something at us, the reflex of avoiding it comes from manas. This function of manas is an instinctual defense mechanism that does not operate on wisdom. But by always trying to defend the self, it can end up destroying the self.

The activity of manas is thinking, cognizing, measuring, reasoning, grasping, and clinging. Day and night, manas discriminates things. "I am this person. You are that person. This is mine. That is yours. This is me. That is you." Pride, anger, fear, and jealousy—mental formations that are based in seeing ourselves as separate—all arise from manas. Because manas is filled with delusion—craving, fear, and clinging—it does not have the capacity to touch the realm of things-in-themselves. It can never touch the realm of suchness of store consciousness. Its object is an image of a self that exists only in the realm of representation. The attachment of manas to a self is based on an image that it has created, just as we fall in love with our image of someone and not with the person herself.

Contact between the six sense bases and the six sense objects may result in the planting of seeds of attachment, craving, anger, hatred, despair, and so on. These seeds may grow to become more important as the same kind of contact continues. They are called internal formations *(samyojana)*, or knots, or fetters. They have the power to bind, to incite, to drive, to push. They deprive us of our liberty and well-being. The planting of these seeds, the formation of these knots, takes place when mindfulness and insight are not there.

Internal formations are not always unpleasant. When we fall in love, the seeds of a sweet formation are sown in our body and mind. Whenever we have a free moment, we want to see our beloved. When we leave our house, even though we may not have the intention of going to her home, we find ourselves driving in that direction. It is as if we cannot help it. The strength of our internal formations pulls us along. That is the seed of craving with attachment. "Attachment" means grasping tightly, clinging blindly. If we touch red ink, our fingers become red. If we are in constant contact with people who are filled with greed, hatred, delusion, and prejudice, some of those characteristics will rub off on us as well and our consciousness will become "stained" by them. Whether bitter or sweet, all mental formations are blocks of suffering in our consciousness. Our internal formations push us to do things that aren't helpful to ourselves or others, yet still we do them. We are propelled by a kind of habit energy, a kind of addiction.

We have the seeds for many kinds of internal formations in our store consciousness. These knots of ignorance, the cravings and afflictions in us, are the forces that shape so much of our behavior and lead us in the direction of suffering. In many Buddhist texts they are called fetters (samyojana) because they hinder our ability to attain peace, joy, and freedom. The base of all these cravings and afflictions is ignorance, our inability to see things clearly. Ignorance is the first element in the cycle of Interdependent Co-Arising. Our lack of understanding leads to volitional actions, which in turn lead us in the direction of sorrow.

Look at someone caught by alcoholism. Every cell in his body, every desire and aspiration, drives him to drink alcohol. That is a volitional force, the kind of energy that determines his life's direction. Our internal formations cause us to crave certain things and to want to go in a certain direction. We may even try to go in another direction, but the blind forces that are pushing us are very strong. They are based in ignorance, in the volitional forces that lie deep in our store consciousness and manifest as our mind/body. Practicing meditation, looking deeply, we can identify and touch the blocks of ignorance, craving, and other afflictions in our store consciousness, and make the right effort to stop going in that direction.

17

Mentation

With store consciousness as its support,
manas arises.
Its function is mentation,
grasping the seeds it considers to be a "self."

MANAS IS CALLED AN EVOLVING, or manifesting consciousness (*paravritti vijñana*) because it comes about as a result of the store consciousness. It does not have an independent self-existence. When studying the Manifestation Only teachings, we need to be careful with this point. Manas is a consciousness—an evolving consciousness based in the store consciousness—but at the same time it is also a base, in this case, the base of the sixth consciousness, mind consciousness.

In Chapter Eight we learned how each of the sense bases, in contact with an object, gives rise to a respective consciousness. The six sense bases are the eyes, ears, nose, tongue, body, and mind. These six sense bases work together with their six sense objects—form, sound, smell, taste, touch, and objects of mind—to give rise to the six sense consciousnesses: eye consciousness, ear consciousness, nose consciousness, tongue consciousness, tactile consciousness, and mind consciousness. Sense base and sense object go together like form and shadow, born simultaneously.

Manas is a sense base for mind consciousness in the same way that the eyes are a sense base for eye consciousness and the ears are a sense base for ear consciousness. However, the objects of mind (thoughts, cognition) do not arise from the external world the way that objects of form, sound, taste, and tactile sensation do. Instead, they come from the working of manas with the seeds in our store consciousness. Without the resulting objects of mind, there would be no mind consciousness, just as without an object of form for the sense base of the eye to contact, there would be no eye consciousness. A consciousness is always consciousness of something. So, we have seven evolving consciousnesses—the six sense consciousnesses and the seventh consciousness, manas—and one root, or base, consciousness, the store consciousness.

When we talk about consciousness, we usually think of it as having two aspects, subject and object. Subject and object are terms used in modern Western philosophy. The Manifestation Only teachings, however, say that every psychological phenomenon has three aspects: a subject (the perceiver, *darshana-bhaga*), an object (the perceived, *nimitta-bhaga*), and the basis that makes both subject and object possible, which is the thing-in-itself (*svabhava-bhaga*).

The German phenomenologist Edmund Husserl stated that consciousness must be consciousness of *something*. In the Manifestation Only teachings, the same point is made. To be angry means to be angry at someone or something. To be sad is to be sad about someone or something. To worry is to worry about something. To think is to think something. All these mental activities *are* consciousness.

When we look at a plate, we see that it has a top and a bottom. The top is not possible without the bottom. Top and bottom are like the perceiver and the perceived aspects of consciousness. We cannot have one without the other. There is also a third aspect—the substance from which the plate is made. If that basic material were not present, there could be no top or bottom, either. Just as we cannot say that the bottom of the plate is not of the same material as the plate itself, we shouldn't discriminate and say that the perceived aspect is not the thing-in-itself aspect. It is also incorrect to say that the bottom of the plate is not the top of the plate. Everything that we know as a plate arises from the basic substance from which it is made, the thing-in-itself that contains the whole.

Perceiver, perceived, and thing-in-itself are together called "the self-revealing aspects" and they depend upon each other. An image found in the sutras to describe this is that of three reeds that are leaning upon and supporting one another. A single reed cannot support anything and it certainly cannot stand by itself. But if you balance three reeds against each other, they will all mutually support one another upright. When we try to separate the three aspects of consciousness—perceiver, perceived, and thing-in-itself—into discrete parts that stand alone, we are going against the Buddha's teaching. Each part contains the other two parts. Each part would not exist without the other parts. Understanding this will help our practice.

The perceived aspect of the store consciousness is the manifestation of the world and the manifestation of the body as a sense base. Everything we perceive—the world of humans, animals, plants, and minerals—is based on the perceived aspect of store consciousness. The instrumental world is the world of nature. The sentient world is the world of all living beings, including humans. Both of these worlds are the object of our perception and they are the perceived aspect of our store consciousness. The subject aspect is what the perceiver, the store consciousness, holds and maintains. In the perceiver are the seeds and formations, which it stores and maintains. Mental formations arise from these seeds in our store consciousness. Every seed and every manifestation lie only in the root of the perceived. The perceiver is also the perceived. The perceived is also the thing-in-itself.

Manas also arises from the thing-in-itself aspect of the store consciousness. It is an evolving consciousness with its roots in the store consciousness. Its function is grasping at store consciousness, which it considers to be a separate entity, a self. The seed of this grasping was already there when we were born and continues to be watered by many things in our social environment. Our seeds of affliction—ignorance, delusion, and craving—manifest themselves as this volitional force called manas.

The object of manas is the perceiver aspect of store consciousness. Just as the perceiver naturally embraces the perceived, manas embraces and clings to this aspect of store consciousness, makes it into an object, and that object becomes an idea of self. All manas does is to think and calculate: "This is me." This is called mentation (*manana*). Day and night, manas is always thinking, believing, grasping, and considering store consciousness as its object, as a separate entity. It is always present as a kind of instinct that takes its object as itself. This perceived object of manas belongs to the field of representations and to the mode of false perception.

The nature of manas is delusion. It is born from the blocks of ignorance that are present as seeds in our store consciousness. It is always there, grasping the idea of self and the idea of nonself. It is always discriminating: this is me, this is mine, this is self; that is not me, that is not mine, that is not self. With or without our conscious awareness, that is the work of manas, and it works continuously.

Manas also believes that "This body is me." If our mind consciousness alone thought this, we could reason with it and dissuade it of this belief. But manas holds this belief very deeply and strongly. Manas believes that if the body disintegrates, the self will disintegrate. And because one of the functions of manas is the instinct to survive, to protect the self, it grasps firmly to its belief that our mind/body is a permanent, never-changing self (*atman*). According to Brahmanic belief, which was the progenitor of Hinduism, the Great Self (*maha-atman*) is an unchanging and indestructible primal source, personified as the god Brahma. Within each of us is a beam of this atman, and salvation means reuniting the small self with the Great Self, with Brahma. This was the dominant belief system in the India of the Buddha's time. The Buddha's teachings on nonself and impermanence were a radical departure from this belief system.

The Buddha offered impermanence as an instrument for us to explore reality and discover the truth of nonself. Just as a flower is made of non-flower elements, the self is made of nonself elements. I am made of non-me elements. When I look deeply, I see the non-me elements that compose me—namely, all of you, all phenomena, and the entire cosmos. But manas is unaware of nonself. It continues to believe in the idea of a permanent, eternal self, and so it is always separating and discriminating between what is self and what is not self. The only way to help manas stop grasping at the notions of self and not-self is for us to practice deep looking into the impermanent and interdependent nature of reality.

18

The Mark of a Self

The object of manas is the mark of a self
found in the field of representations
at the point where manas
and store consciousness touch.

WE HAVE ALREADY DISCUSSED the three fields of perception—the realm of things-in-themselves, the realm of representations, and the realm of mere images—and the three modes of perception: direct, by inference or deduction, and false. The mode of perception of the realm of things-in-themselves is always immediate and direct, with no reasoning or calculating. In manas, the mode of perception belongs to the realm of representations. The Chinese character for "representation" means "carries with it some of the substance." For "the beloved," the Chinese use an expression that means "the person in the mind." Xuanzang, in his *Standard Verses on the Eight Consciousnesses*, says, "The object of manas is the realm of representations, and the nature of that world is obscuration." Because manas is obscured, it loves blindly. The object of the "love" of manas that manas holds on to so tightly is not the reality of store consciousness, but an image that manas has created.

The object of the lover's perception is linked both to the lover, manas, and the thing-in-itself, the store consciousness. When manas and store consciousness are in contact, their two energies bring about an object at the point where manas and store consciousness meet and overlap. It cannot touch things directly. It arises from the ground of store consciousness, touches a part of it, produces an image of it, and takes this image as an object of its perception. It regards this perceived object as a self and falls in love with it. Then it has to protect this part of store consciousness that it has objectified and attached to.

In order to transform manas, we need to look deeply at the elements of ignorance and craving that cause it to act in this way. The roots of manas lie in our store consciousness. Looking deeply into manas, we can identify the seeds of ignorance and the internal formations of craving and afflictions that are there, which are held in our store consciousness. It is like looking into an orange and being able to see the orange tree that will grow from the seeds. Manas is "obscured," covered by a veil of ignorance. Does this mean that it should be eliminated? No. Manas has store consciousness in it, and store consciousness contains everything, including Buddha nature.

In fact, all eight consciousnesses and all mental formations have the nature of interbeing and interpenetration. They are both collective and individual. Even though manas is blind and its functioning creates so much suffering for us, all the other consciousnesses are at the same time present in it. If we try to eliminate manas, it would be like destroying ourselves. In the flower we can see the sun, the compost, and the earth. One thing brings with it all other things. One thing is all things. When we practice looking like this, we will not complain about manas and how it is always causing us to suffer. In Buddhism, there are no external enemies—there is only ourselves. The object of manas is just a representation, an image in our minds, not something real outside of us. When we understand better how manas brings about this false object of perception, we will be able to learn how to practice to avoid this.

The Manifestation Only teachings and other schools of Buddhism describe four conditions for the manifestation of all phenomena. The first is cause as condition (hetu-pratyaya). The Chinese character for this term has the ideogram for "great" inside a square. Even though the cause itself is limiting, the result can nevertheless be significant. A single grain of wheat gives rise to an entire wheat plant.

The second condition is condition for development (adhipati-pratyaya). There are two kinds of conditions for development: those favorable for development and those that hinder development. Sunshine, rain, and soil can either help or not help a grain of wheat become a wheat plant, depending on the timing, amount, and quality of each. If it rains too much or at the wrong time, the plant will not flourish. Not all unfavorable conditions, however, bring about an unwholesome result. Perhaps we are on the brink of making a mistake but, thanks to unfavorable conditions, we avoid doing something destructive. In this case, the so-called adverse conditions were actually beneficial. They hindered the development of a harmful action.

The third condition is object as condition (alambana-pratyaya). "Object" here means the object of perception. Without that object, there is no perception. One of the Buddha's most devoted lay followers was the merchant Anathapindika. He first learned of the Buddha from his brother-in-law, who was a disciple of the Buddha. When Anathapindika heard the name "Buddha," an image arose in his mind and he felt great love for the Buddha. But he had never actually seen the Buddha, so the image in his mind belonged to the realm of representations. This representation (his image of the Buddha) served as the object as condition, which in turn relied on the condition for development (the way Anathapindika's brother-in-law spoke of the Buddha and prepared for his arrival.) Later, when Anathapindika was able to come into direct contact with the Buddha, the object condition for his perception of the Buddha became closer to the truth.

The fourth condition is the condition of immediate continuity (samanantara-pratyaya). Every manifestation of a phenomenon needs continuity or it is cut off. The flower of this moment needs the flower of the previous moment in order to exist. Nothing can exist without immediate continuity.

For anything to be born or for any phenomenon to manifest, it needs these four conditions. Our ideas of cause and effect are quite oversimplified. The cause as condition (hetu-pratyaya) is the seed from which things arise, but nothing can arise from this alone. There also has to be a development-condition (adhipati-pratyaya), an object condition (alambana-pratyaya), and the condition of immediate continuity (samanantara-pratyaya). If I had not been in the previous moment, I could not now be in this moment.

The cause as condition of manas is the thing-in-itself aspect of store consciousness. Manas is born from a seed of coveting a portion of the store consciousness. The condition for development of manas is the perceiver aspect of store consciousness. Manas is determined to hold on to the perceiver aspect of store consciousness. Based on this, manas creates an object of its perception. But the perceiver aspect of store consciousness is not a direct object of manas and so this condition is not a direct object condition of manas. Instead, manas relies on the perceiver aspect of store consciousness to create its own special object condition. The perceiver aspect of the store consciousness is the favorable condition for development of the wrong perception of manas, the false perception of reality that manas covets as its beloved. This is like encountering someone in a dream and believing that person to be real.

During the night, our mind is subjected to the will of manas. In sleep, we live not in the realm of representation but in the realm of mere images. While we are sleeping, manas urges our mind consciousness to make use of the seeds in store consciousness to create an environment that satisfies the desires of manas. Our mind consciousness produces dreams that are made up of images from seeds in our store consciousness. But a dream-person is not a real person. In the same way, the object of manas is not the real perceiver aspect of our store consciousness. The real perceiver aspect of store consciousness plays the role of the condition for development on which manas is based in order to develop an object condition, which is its wrong perception. Manas creates this false image of a beloved one by basing itself on conditions that are favorable for this kind of creation. It arises due to the impulse of ignorance and craving from seeds in the store consciousness.

In the Mahayana-samgraha-shastra and in the Lankavatara Sutra, store consciousness is compared to the ocean and the seven evolving consciousnesses are compared to waves. This is how we can identify the roots of manas. Manas looks at store consciousness with attachment and makes a portion of it into an object that it can cling to. When this happens, store consciousness is caught and cannot be free. The object of manas is made possible by the contact and overlap of manas and store consciousness. But this object is not the thing-in-itself, it is only a representation. It is merely a composite of the subject of store consciousness and manas, related a tiny bit to the original substance of store consciousness, which is suchness.

Consciousness has many functions. Every function of consciousness is a psychological reality. When we speak about eight consciousnesses, we are really talking about eight functions of consciousness. If we try to divide consciousness into eight independent entities, we are going against the spirit of Buddhist teachings, in which everything is intimately linked with everything else. We think that store consciousness and manas are different, but there is an intimate connection between the two. They are two, but they are also one.

I am called Thich Nhat Hanh. I am a Dharma teacher, a poet, and a gardener. The poet part of me is not separate from the Dharma teacher part of me, and the Dharma teacher is not separate from the gardener. Each of us has many facets. We can analyze and see the basis of each facet, but this does not mean that any facet is independent of the others. They are merely different aspects of a whole.

Consciousness is the same. The eight consciousnesses are not eight separate entities that have nothing to do with each other. Different functions of consciousness are given different names, but those functions are closely linked with each other. Although they are eight, they are also one. When we say that the first function of consciousness is to store the seeds, we give this function a name, "store consciousness," and then we have an idea of a store consciousness. When we are discussing the second function of consciousness, thinking and calculating, we call this function manas. The second function is naturally linked to and influenced by the first. The function of poet is linked to and influenced by that of gardener. The function of gardener is linked to and influenced by the function of Dharma teacher. The true poet contains the gardener, and the true gardener contains the teacher.

The object of manas is the mark of a self, found in the realm of representations, created at the point where manas and store consciousness touch. At that point, the object called "self" appears. It is a product of the constructed mind, based on ignorance and delusion. It is part of the realm of representations and not the realm of suchness, or things-in-themselves. It is only something that has been constructed by our deluded mind, just as when we mistake a rope for a snake.

Store consciousness is like the ocean. The evolving consciousnesses are like waves. When we understand this, when we remember the intimate relationship between manas and store consciousness, we will not revile manas. Instead we will work toward transforming the seeds in our store consciousness so that they manifest in a wholesome way and not as the false perceptions of manas.

19

Discrimination

As the ground of wholesome and unwholesome
of the other six manifesting consciousnesses,
manas continues discriminating.
Its nature is both indeterminate and obscured.

MANAS IS THE BASIS for determining whether the other six manifesting consciousnesses—the sense consciousnesses of eye, ear, nose, tongue, body, and mind—are wholesome or unwholesome. The sense consciousnesses are heavily influenced by manas. If manas is obscured and confused, they are obscured and confused. If manas is partially liberated, they will be partially liberated. If manas loves in a blind and confused way, the other six consciousnesses will suffer. The greater the blindness of manas, the greater the blindness of the sense consciousnesses. When manas opens itself and becomes more accepting, these six consciousnesses also enjoy openness and acceptance. That is why manas is called "the ground of wholesome and unwholesome." In order to transform manas, we have to transform our store consciousness, which holds all the seeds that are the base for manas.

The other six consciousnesses stop operating from time to time, but manas, like the store consciousness, is continuous. Manas goes on working day and night. Unlike store consciousness, which is continuous but does not discriminate, the nature of manas is both continuous and discriminating. To say that manas is always discriminating means that it holds on to the object that it regards as its self, its beloved. Everything in the world is connected with us yet we think, "Those things are not myself. Only this is myself." We generally think that our actions are rational, that only when we understand something do we act. But this is not always so.

We have some understanding, but often our emotions are stronger than our reasoning.

The nature of manas is indeterminate, like store consciousness. But it is also obscured by ignorance. "Obscured" means to be "covered up." You cannot see the light if there is something covering it up. "Ignorance" in Sanskrit is avidya—literally, the absence of knowledge (vidya). The veil of ignorance that covers manas is the tendency to discriminate between self and nonself. Indeterminate means neither wholesome nor unwholesome. This means that there is a possibility of transformation from clinging and discriminating to letting go and nondiscrimination. The transformation of manas can happen because it is indeterminate. The earth can give rise to thorns and brambles, but it can also give rise to fragrant fruits and flowers.

The nature of store consciousness is unobstructed, which means it can become true mind, Buddha nature. There is no obstacle standing in its way. There is the possibility of reaching the realm of things-in-themselves. Transformation occurs in the store consciousness. When the seeds from which manas has evolved are transformed, manas will be transformed. Then the discrimination between self and nonself, mine and not mine, will vanish.

The goal of meditation is to make a change at the root of manas and the store consciousness. This is called transformation at the base (ashraya paravritti). Paravritti means "revolution." Revolution means turning and going in a different direction. Ashraya is "base." Only with the light of mindfulness can this radical transformation take place. Through mindfulness, we can turn and go in the direction of awakening. Our practice is to transform the nature of manas a little bit each day and release our store consciousness more and more from its grip.

The root of manas is delusion, the seeds of ignorance that lie deep in our store consciousness. The highest task of mind consciousness is to shine the light of mindfulness on manas and the seeds in our store consciousness, allowing us to see them. When our mind consciousness projects light on to these seeds, touching them deeply with mindfulness, it penetrates the blocks of delusion and helps them to be transformed. When illuminated by the light of mindfulness, delusions are less able to manifest in unwholesome acts of our body, speech, and mind. Delusion operates in darkness but not in light. When these blocks of ignorance are transformed, manas is transformed.

Our mind consciousness does not have to work directly with manas. It can work with the seeds in store consciousness. Store consciousness is like a garden, a plot of earth that contains all the seeds. A garden cannot cultivate itself. A gardener is needed. When the gardener has plowed, hoed, tilled, sown the seeds, and watered the earth, the earth offers flowers and fruits to support the life of the gardener. The gardener knows that it is not he that brings forth the fruits, but the earth itself. His job is simply to take care of the earth. Through mindfulness, mind consciousness touches the fetters of delusion and craving, the blocks of suffering that are in the store consciousness. This is done day and night, like a gardener working nonstop. In this way, mind consciousness helps the store consciousness bring forth the fruit of the practice—joy, peace, and transformation.

When we use our mind consciousness to generate the energy of mindfulness by practicing mindful breathing or walking, we water the seed of mindfulness that is already present in our store consciousness. This generates even more energy of mindfulness that can shine even further into the store consciousness. When we use the energy of mindfulness to touch other seeds, we help those seeds transform. When mindfulness touches beautiful, positive seeds, it helps these seeds develop and reveal themselves more clearly. When it touches negative seeds, it helps those seeds to transform.

When we come to a practice center, we bring our store consciousness and manas with us, and we receive seeds of the Dharma. Our mind consciousness sows these seesds in our store consciousness. We cannot hold the seeds of the Dharma in our intellect, our mind consciousness. We have to bring the teachings into our whole person and plant them in the soil of our store consciousness. Then, day and night, while walking, sitting, eating, drinking, in all our activities we water those seeds with our mindfulness.

We can have confidence in our store consciousness. Store consciousness never ceases its activity. During the night, our mind consciousness may rest and stop functioning, but our store consciousness continues to work. After the gardener stops working, the soil continues to work in order to help the seeds sprout and grow. Sooner or later, quite naturally, we will have a breakthrough. The flowers and fruits of awakening will arise from our store consciousness. Mind consciousness has to trust store consciousness, just as a gardener has to trust the land. Both roles are important. Remember, though, that enlightenment, insight, will be brought to you not by mind consciousness, not through your intellectual understanding, but through the deeper wisdom of your store consciousness. After transformation, store consciousness becomes the Great Mirror Wisdom, shining forth and illuminating everything.

For awakening to flower, we have to sow the seed of awakening in our store consciousness. If we only use our mind consciousness for mental gymnastics, we won't go very far. Many people keep the teachings they learn up in their mind consciousness, using their intellect to poke and prod at them. Even though they think about them and talk about them all the time, they never learn how to bring the seeds of the Dharma into their store consciousness and entrust them to the fertile soil.

If you practice meditation with your mind consciousness alone, you can never succeed. Don't think or reason too much about the things you learn from a meditation teacher. Instead, sow the Dharma seeds in your store consciousness. Then, in your everyday life, whether you are walking, standing, lying down, sitting, cooking, or working at a computer, water those seeds with mindfulness. Your store consciousness, your plot of land, will allow these Dharma seeds to germinate and the flower of awakening to grow.

In Chapter Eleven, we learned about the Three Dharma Seals of nonself, impermanence, and nirvana. Another way to describe nirvana is interbeing. Contemplating the nonself, impermanent, and interdependent nature of phenomena can help us reduce the amount of delusion in manas and bring us closer to the wisdom of nondiscrimination. This is the kind of wisdom that can help us see into the true nature of interbeing. There is no separation between "this" and "that." With good practice, the delusion of manas can be transformed into the wisdom of equanimity.

20

Companions of Manas

Manas goes with the five universals,
with mati of the five particulars,
and with the four major and eight secondary afflictions.
All are indeterminate and obscured.

MANY OF THE FIFTY-ONE mental formations operate together with manas.[18] Manas goes with the five universals: contact, attention, feelings, perception, and volition. They are called universal because they are present in every consciousness The function of always thinking, which belongs to manas, manifests as these five universals. Manas is always in contact, being attentive, feeling, perceiving, and intending. Through the activity of these five universal mental formations, manas grasps the store consciousness and regards it as a self. The function of always thinking, which belongs to manas, is manifested in these five universals. It is always in contact, being attentive, feeling, perceiving, and intending. This is how manas grasps the store consciousness and pretends that it is its self.

The five particular mental formations (viniyata) are not found at all times in every consciousness. They are: zeal (chanda), determination (adhimoksha), mindfulness or remembering (smrti), concentration (samadhi), and wisdom (prajña). The first of these five particulars, zeal, contains the qual-

18 The fifty-one categories are the five universal, the five particular, the eleven wholesome, the twenty-six unwholesome, and the four indeterminate mental formations. The unwholesome mental formations are further divided into two kinds: the six root unwholesome formations and the twenty secondary unwholesome formations. The six root unwholesome mental formations are the most poisonous states of mind. They are: greed (*raga*), hatred (*dosa*), ignorance (*moha*), arrogance (*mana*), doubt (*vichikitsa*), and false views (*drishti*). All fifty-one categories of mental formations are detailed in chap. 30. For more on mental formations, see Thich Nhat Hanh, *The Heart of the Buddha's Teaching*, chaps. 11 and 23.

ity of attraction. You are drawn to look at something, to know about it, to be interested in it. The second, determination, can also be described as discernment—you think you have recognized the object, you form an idea of it. The third, mindfulness, means in this context that the object of your attention has come to exist in the here and now for you; you recall it and it is as if it were real. Concentration, here, means that you focus your attention on that object. The meaning of wisdom, here, is that you believe you know exactly what the object is.

The Sanskrit terms for these five particular mental formations can be confusing because in different contexts they have different meanings. In particular, "prajña," which is the only one of the five particulars found in manas, is not the same prajña of *prajñaparamita*, true insight. Here it means a kind of understanding or conviction that is only an idea, an assertion. It is not pure wisdom. In fact, it is often based in a wrong perception—you believe you are right, but you are wrong. You think you have seen a snake, but it was only a rope.

Very often we cling to one thing that we think to be reality. We have a strong conviction that it is the absolute truth and we will not be budged from that conviction. This is why even "prajña" is here called the wrong kind of insight. Let us reserve the word "prajña" for true understanding, true insight, and instead use for this particular mental formation the word *mati*, which means an understanding that might be false. When we perceive something, even if we perceive it wrongly, we have the impression that we are right. We see something, grasp it, and say that it is the unalterable truth. Manas says the "self" it has created as an object of its perception is the most important thing. This insight is obscured—it is mati, a strongly held, false perception.

The Buddha taught a parable that illustrates this kind of thinking. A man, the father of a little boy, went away for a few days, leaving his son at home. When he returned, he found that his house had been burned down by bandits. He saw the charred remains of a child lying near the ruins of the house. Immediately he believed that this was the body of his little boy, and he threw himself on the ground and beat his chest in grief. The next day he organized a funeral ceremony, collected the ashes, and put them into a beautiful silk bag. This man was very attached to his little boy, and he carried the bag of ashes with him wherever he went. He didn't know that his son was still alive, that he had been captured by the bandits.

Some time later, the boy was able to escape. In the middle of the night he reached the house his father had rebuilt. When he knocked and asked his father to open the door, the man, convinced that his son was dead, became very angry. He yelled, "Go away. Don't disturb me. My son is dead." The child tried again and again to convince his father that he was his son, but the man's conviction that his son was dead was so strong that he would not listen. Finally the boy gave up and went away.

Sometimes we cling to what we believe so much that even when the truth comes and knocks at our door, we refuse to let it in. This kind of blind conviction in our own beliefs—fanaticism—is the enemy of practice. We should never be absolutely certain of our knowledge. We need to be ready to give it up at a moment's notice for a higher truth. This is called nonattachment to views, and it is one of the most important elements of our practice. Any view, no matter how noble or beautiful, even our belief in Buddhism, can be a trap. Remember, the Buddha warned that his teaching is like a snake—if we don't know the proper way to receive the teachings, we will be caught by them. We will be bitten by the snake.

The twentieth verse also mentions the afflictions (klesha) with which manas is associated. Afflictions are unwholesome mental formations. The four major afflictions mentioned in this verse all have to do with ideas about the self. They are self-ignorance (*atma-moha*), self-view (*atma-drishti*), self-pride (*atma-mano*), and self-love (*atma-sneha*). Self-ignorance is a wrong idea of the self, such as the belief that "I am this body, I am this feeling, I am this perception. Things that are not this body, this feeling, this perception, are not me. Things that happen to others are of no concern to me." In fact, what we call "I" is linked to everything else in the universe. If we take a tiny particle and create an image of that reality and call it a self, that is not the real self but only the sign of a self in the realm of representations. It does not belong to the realm of things-in-themselves, and so it is said to be "ignorant regarding the self."

Self-view is the false view that the self is independent and eternal, that it exists apart from other factors of existence. Self-pride is the attitude that we are better, more intelligent, more beautiful, or more important than others.

Self-love is when we love ourselves excessively, when everything we say, do, or think shows how caught up with ourselves we are. These four major afflictions are always present in manas. Our practice is to shine the light on manas so that it can release its belief in the self.

The secondary afflictions mentioned in this verse are less grievous than these false notions of self. They are further divided into the greater secondary afflictions, the middle secondary afflictions, and the lesser secondary afflictions. Manas is associated with the eight greater secondary afflictions of anger, enmity, concealment or hypocrisy, affliction or vexation, envy, parsimony or selfishness, deception or deceit, and fraudulence or dishonesty.

These unwholesome mental formations, whether universal or particular, bear the same kind of nature. They are all indeterminate and obscured, exactly like manas. The ocean is salty, so all the drops of water in the ocean are also salty at the same time. Mental formations take on the characteristics of the consciousness with which they are associated. Because manas is obscured by ignorance and is indeterminate, all the mental formations that go along with it have the same nature: obscured and indeterminate. And because they are indeterminate, they can be transformed.

21

Shadow Follows Form

As shadow follows form,
manas always follows store.
It is a misguided attempt to survive,
craving for continuation and blind satisfaction.

MANAS ALWAYS FOLLOWS the store consciousness like our shadow follows the movements of our body. In this way, manas is blind, blindly following whatever seeds it latches onto in the store consciousness, whether they are wholesome or unwholesome. But the unwholesome always contains within itself the potential of the wholesome, according to the teaching of interbeing, just as the flower can be seen in the garbage and the garbage can be seen in the flower. That is why transformation and awakening are possible. When manas is awakened, when it has been transformed, it has the wonderful function called the understanding of equality (*samata jñana*), which means the ability to see the one in the all and the all in the one.

Earlier, I mentioned the function of manas as our "survival instinct." Because it is attached to the idea of self, it always acts to preserve the self. When we are sleeping and something startles us, that reaction is due to manas. When someone tries to hit us and we move to avoid the blow, that rapid self-protective response belongs to manas. Mind consciousness has not had enough time to consider the situation and set an action into motion, but manas behaves automatically, instinctively. This capacity of manas is akin to what biologists call the "primitive" brain, which functions solely in the interest of survival, of self-preservation.

Whenever we are in any situation of great danger, manas works hard, persuading us to run or to do whatever is necessary to save our life. But because manas is blind, because its nature is obscured by delusion, it can often take us in the wrong direction. To describe the potentially self-destructive aspect of the "survival instinct," modern psychology uses the image of a snake that has a mosquito on it. In order to get rid of the mosquito, the snake lies in the road so a car will drive over it—killing the mosquito but also the snake. Human beings also act like this. We want to punish someone, so we destroy ourselves in order to make the other person suffer. Manas is the force behind this kind of thinking.

Because of its clinging to the notion of a "self," manas is defensive and protective. It has the blind instinct of self-preservation, always craving for a permanent self, for satisfaction. Mind consciousness can practice deep touching and deep looking in order to be in touch with reality. The nature of manas is delusion, ignorance, and discrmination. It is imprisoned in its delusion and its craving for duration and satisfaction. Manas seeks to satisfy craving, even when doing so might be unhealthy. It drives us in the direction of attaining pleasure, but it often turns out to be the kind of pleasure that does not actually bring happiness. But because manas does not see where it is going, the fruits of its journey are often more painful than happy, more sad than joyful.

22

Release

When the first stage of the bodhisattva path is attained,
the obstacles of knowledge and afflictions are transformed.
At the tenth stage, the yogi transforms the belief in a separate self,
and store consciousness is released from manas.

ACCORDING TO THE TEACHINGS of Mahayana Buddhism, there are ten stages (*bhumi*) a bodhisattva has to go through before attaining full enlightenment.[19] The first is the stage of joy (*pramudita-bhumi*). As we begin to practice, we experience great joy because we have been able to put an end to the noise, the demands, and the stressful activities of everyday life. We feel the joy of releasing things and leaving them behind. The more you are capable of releasing, the more joyful you become. You think that this or that is essential for your happiness, but if you let these notions go you will discover that they were really obstacles to your happiness. In the first stage we are able to let go of many of the things that have been imprisoning us and we feel a great sense of relief. But, as a bodhisattva, we cannot stay there. If we are attached to the stage of joy and just want to remain there for our own pleasure, we will not be able to go far on the bodhisattva path.

When a bodhisattva enters the first stage, he or she realizes the transformation of obstacles. There are two kinds of obstacles: obstacles of knowledge (*jñeya-avarana*) and obstacles of afflictions (*klesha-avarana*). According to Buddhist thought, when we know something, when we learn something, it can become an obstacle to our progress. If we cling to what we have learned as the absolute truth, we are caught by that knowledge.

19 See Thich Nhat Hanh, *Interbeing: Fourteen Guidelines for Engaged Buddhism*, Third Edition (Berkeley, CA: Parallax Press, 1998).

For this reason, we have to be very careful about what we know. It may be an obstacle to our transformation, our happiness. Acquiring knowledge is like climbing a ladder: in order to step up to a higher rung we have to let go of the rung we are standing on. If we believe that the step we are standing on is the highest, then we can climb no higher.

The technique of learning in this tradition is always to release, to let go of what we have just learned, of what we have already obtained. Never believe that what you know is absolute truth. This is reflected in the First Mindfulness Training of the Order of Interbeing. If you are caught by the knowledge you presently possess, that is the end of your progress. If scientists cling to what they already know, they will not be able to discover other truths. They must be able to drop what they know about something the moment they learn something new that contradicts or supercedes it. On the path of practice, knowledge is an obstacle that must be overcome. We must be ready to abandon our knowledge at any moment in order to get to a higher level of understanding. This is very important.

At the first stage, we have already begun to put an end to both the affliction-obstacle and the knowledge-obstacle. The knowledge-obstacle occurs more in the realm of the intellect, while the affliction-obstacle is more in the realm of the emotions. Our envy, hatred, anger, sadness, despair, and anxiety are all obstacles of afflictions. If our sadness is so great that we feel paralyzed, that is an affliction-obstacle. If we are depressed, suffering too much, or desiring too much, these are all obstacles to our practice.

Our ignorance and inability to see the truth belong to the knowledge-obstacle. This means that the way we see things is not the way things are—just like the mati of manas, an understanding or conviction that may be false. Our point of view, perception, and learning are all the objects of our knowledge, and these are the things that prevent us from going ahead. "I already know everything there is to know about that. I don't need to learn any more." We have arrived only at the fourth rung of the ladder, yet we think it is the top rung. Whatever the value of what our intellect and our insight has attained, we have to abandon it. If we don't, we put an end to further progress. Even though it has some value, our knowledge has become an obstacle. If we are caught in our knowledge, if we say that our knowledge is absolute truth, we suffer from the knowledge-obstacle. Those who have knowledge but know that they have to abandon it in order to go further do not suffer from the knowledge-obstacle.

Objects of knowledge are like water that has become ice and prevents the river from flowing. We need knowledge, but we have to use it intelligently. When we think that our present knowledge is paramount, our way ahead is blocked. Our knowledge has become an obstacle. This way of looking at knowledge is quite special to Buddhism. The Buddha taught that we cannot be attached to anything; we have to abandon even our insight, our understanding, and our knowledge.

Knowledge-obstacles are easier to abolish than affliction-obstacles. Affliction-obstacles need more time, more practice, to dissolve. Our anger, misery, and despair are blocks in our store consciousness. We have to practice touching them deeply with the energy of mindfulness in order to see their roots and transform them. Solidity is important for our well-being. When you practice walking meditation, each step you take in mindfulness should help you cultivate a little bit more solidity and freedom. When craving, anger, or jealousy manifest as mental formations in your mind consciousness, it is like having a fever. It burns. But in the first stage, the stage of joy, the bodhisattva begins to remove the obstacles of knowledge and affliction and experiences just the opposite—a state of being refreshed.

When the bodhisattva arrives at the eighth stage, the belief in an innate self is transformed. This stage is called the Realm of the Immovable (*achalabhumi*). When you arrive at this stage on the bodhisattva path, the deep-seated belief in a separate self vanishes, and at that instant the grip of manas on the store consciousness is released. There is liberation from the belief in a separate self. Before this, even though we may have been able to obtain some intellectual knowledge of nonself, our belief in a self was still deeply rooted in manas. It is almost innate in us. That is why we have to practice until we arrive at the eighth stage of the bodhisattva in order to uproot this belief. Then store consciousness is released and becomes the Great Mirror Wisdom.

There are two kinds of attachment to self. One is the habit of attachment that we acquire in this life, the other is the attachment that we already had when we were born. Here, the verse is referring to the second kind. The attachment to self has been in existence for a long time, carried as seeds in the store consciousness from lifetime to lifetime. When the bodhisattva arrives at the eighth stage, the Realm of the Immovable, she transforms the innate belief in a separate self, and manas becomes the Wisdom of Equality. All the blocks of discrimination, ignorance, and craving about the self have been transformed, thanks to the practice of looking deeply activated by our mind consciousness.

When this takes place, manas is transformed. Before this transformation, manas was the energy of grasping and discriminating. Now it becomes a kind of wisdom that can perceive the true nature of interbeing. There is no longer any discrimination between self and nonself; you are me, and I am you. We inter-are. There is no boundary between us. In this stage, the bodhisattva realizes his nature of interbeing and the nature of interbeing of all phenomena. The capacity to see and to live accordingly is the wisdom of equality.

Seeds are produced and strengthened by formations. Formations are manifestations of seeds. Not only mental formations come from the seeds in our store consciousness, but physical and physiological formations also are manifestations from seeds in our store consciousness. All manifestations in the eighteen realms: the six realms of the sense organs, the six realms of sense objects, and the six realms of sense consciousnesses, come from the seeds in our store consciousness. Meditators learn to investigate the true nature of these manifestations and see them not as real entities but as conventional designations (*prajñapti* or *samketa*). They are the objects of our cognition, our concepts, our notions, our metaphors, our appellations, our language. Therefore the planting and the growth of all the seeds operating in our daily life can be called the "impregnation of language." Besides the "impregnation of language," there is the "impregnation of selfhood," which means the cultivation of the idea of self or the tendency of appropriation. Store consciousness is also described as the "appropriating consciousness" because not only does it uphold all the sense organs, sense objects, and sense consciousnesses, but it is also the support for taking up all future existences and manifestations. And because seeds of rebirth are being planted and watered in our daily life, a third aspect of impregnation is also going on. This is the "impregnation of samsara"—namely, the twelve links of causation called nidana or pratitya-samutpada. With the practice of mindfulness, concentration, and looking deeply, it is possible to reverse this tendency. The capacity of looking at formations as only conventional designations, the capacity to see them as having no separate selves, and the capacity to transform our attachment and craving will take us in the direction of liberation and healing.

PART III

Mind Consciousness

THE NEXT FIVE VERSES, Twenty-Three through Twenty-Seven, describe the nature and characteristics of the sixth consciousness, mind consciousness (*manovijñana*). As we have learned, manas is the base of mind consciousness, and because the mode of perception of manas is always erroneous, much of what we perceive in our mind consciousness is also false. Because the nature of manas is obscured, our mind consciousness is often also covered over by delusion. Unlike manas, however, our mind consciousness is capable of other modes of perception as well—direct or inferred. When our mind consciousness is able to perceive things directly, it is capable of touching the realm of suchness.

The way to train our mind consciousness in correct perception is through mindfulness. This is the most important contribution of the mind consciousness. When we are mindful, when we are aware of all our actions of body, speech, and mind, we can choose to act, speak, and think in wholesome ways rather than in harmful ways. With the energy of mindfulness generated by our mind consciousness, we can avoid watering seeds of anger, craving, and delusion in our store consciousness and we can water seeds of joy, peace, and wisdom. This is why it is so important to train our mind consciousness in the habit of mindfulness.

23

Sphere of Cognition

With manas as its base
and phenomena as its objects,
mind consciousness manifests itself.
Its sphere of cognition is the broadest.

As we have learned, a consciousness is born when a base has contact with an object. The first five consciousnesses are associated with the faculties of our sense perceptions, and all have a sense organ as their base—eye, ear, nose, tongue, and body. With manas as its base and all phenomena as its objects, mind consciousness manifests itself. Mind consciousness has the capacity to reach out into every direction. The object of mind consciousness can include everything in the eighteen realms. Everything that we can see, hear, smell, taste, touch, or think can be an object of our mind consciousness. Its sphere of perception is the entire cosmos. Manas has the function of thinking, imagining, cognizing, perceiving, and sensing everything—all mental and physical phenomena (dharmas) can be the objects of its perception. Mental phenomena are ideas, notions, and thoughts. "Mountain" as an idea or a concept is an object of mind consciousness.

Many kinds of conditions are needed to bring something into manifestation. There are two primary conditions—sense base and sense object. Both have to be present for a phenomenon to arise. Even though manas is its base, the seed cause-condition of the mind consciousness does not lie in manas but in the store consciousness. Manas is like an electrical conduit between the store consciousness and the mind consciousness, but because its nature is obscured, it distorts the electrical signal, the information, passing between store consciousness and mind consciousness. When mind consciousness is able to touch the seeds in store consciousness directly, without the distortion of manas, it is capable of touching the realm of suchness.

Store consciousness is the garden, mind consciousness the gardener. The gardener has faith in the earth and entrusts to it seeds he considers to be important. Store consciousness has the power to maintain, nourish, and bring forth what we expect to have. In the practice of meditation, we trust our store consciousness. We plant seeds in the soil of our store consciousness, and we water those seeds. We trust that one day the seeds will sprout and bring forth plants, flowers, and fruit.

24

Perception

Mind consciousness has three modes of perception.
It has access to the three fields of perception and is capable
of having three natures.
All mental formations manifest in it—
universal, particular, wholesome, unwholesome and indeterminate.

IN PART ONE, we discussed the three modes of perception and the three fields of perception. Let's review them here to better understand how they function with mind consciousness. The three modes of perception (pramana) are direct perception (pratyaksha pramana), inference (anumana pramana), and wrong direct perception or wrong inference, which results in wrong perception (abhava pramana).

The first mode, direct perception, does not require an intermediary or deduction. When you put your fingers into a flame, you get burned. You feel the heat. That is direct perception—and correct perception. Sometimes you have a direct perception but it is not correct. For example, you see a snake. There's no thinking, no comparison—you just see a snake right away, directly. But then you discover that it is not a snake but only a piece of rope. This is a direct perception that isn't correct, and so it belongs to the third mode, false perception.

The second mode of perception is inference. It is discursive, speculative, and deductive. This mode of perception can also be correct or incorrect. For example, suppose you are standing about ten yards away from a pile of wood. You see smoke rising from behind the wood and so you infer that there is a fire there. That is perception by inference—and it may be true. You are there, and you really see smoke. But sometimes the inference, the deduction, is wrong. It may be smoke from a wood fire, or it may be exhaust from an automobile, or there may be someone smoking a cigarette nearby, and there is no fire at all. So in that case, it is a wrong inference, a wrong perception, and it too belongs to the third mode of perception.

The third mode of perception is the wrong perception that may be the result of either direct perception or inference. If what we perceive or deduce is not the thing-as-it-is, the mode of perception is wrong. Direct perception may be either correct or incorrect. Inference may also be correct or incorrect. When they are incorrect, they are classified as wrong perceptions. Mind consciousness has the capability of all three modes of perception. It is capable of perceiving things directly, by inference, and erroneously either directly or by inference. But for manas, the first evolving consciousness and the base of mind consciousness, the mode of perception is always this third mode—wrong perception. Manas always sees as self things that are not self. With manas as its base, our mind consciousness can easily get caught in wrong perceptions.

Our perceptions are brought about by many causes and conditions, essential and secondary. In fact, our ideas about things are usually nothing more than reminiscences. The Buddha may have been the first person to teach that ideas are just a habit of memory. The Ekottara Agama says that most of our perceptions are the result of recalling things in the past. So often when we perceive something we're merely perceiving an old seed in our store consciousness. This perception has nothing to do with the real object in the here and now. Due to manas, even when the truth is new and fresh, we cannot touch it. We touch only the seeds in our own consciousness.

We seldom have a true direct perception or a true inference. Our usual way of seeing is false perception. A southerner has ideas about northerners. These ideas could come from books he has read or from what he has heard people say. Suppose he meets someone whom he has been told is a northerner. Because he already has an idea about what a northerner is, that idea prevents him from seeing the actual person standing before him. His idea is an obstacle that prevents him from understanding the person as he really is. He has not touched the real person of the northerner, but is only able to touch his own ideas about northerners.

We all have ideas of what a northerner is like, what a southerner is like, what someone from the midlands is like. We have our categories, and we put the northerner into one of them, the southerner into another, and the person from the midlands into a third one. We are all victims of this kind of perception. We have a set of containers in our store consciousness, and when we perceive something, we place it into one of those containers. But our way of placing things into containers is confused. There is a container for licorice, but we put cinnamon into it. We say it is licorice and we believe that it is licorice, so we put it into the box for licorice, but in fact it is cinnamon.

The inference mode needs reflection. If we know how to reflect in a skillful way, it can lead to seeing the truth. Based on findings from a dig, archaeologists attempt to reconstruct the daily lives of people who lived in former times. It might be an accurate reconstruction or a false one. The French philosopher and anthropologist Claude Lévi-Strauss pointed out that a scientist could go to a place that has never been inhabited by civilized people, dig down into the earth, find a typewriter, and conclude that five or six thousand years ago there were people living in that place who had the technology of the typewriter. Even if we have the appropriate training and credentials, we have not come to the right conclusion. This is a wrong mode of inference.

Often when we are suspicious of someone it is because of wrong inference. Imagine a young boy who has received a wristwatch for his birthday. He goes swimming and when he comes out of the pool, his watch stays behind. He thinks, "Yesterday, when I received the gift, my best friend was there. He seemed envious and the look in his eyes showed that he wanted it." Based on this idea, the boy concludes that his friend must have stolen his watch, though he has not explored other possibilities for the watch's disappearance. If this were the right conclusion, it would be a true mode of inference. But it is the wrong conclusion, and so it is a false mode of inference.

Our perceptions and our inferences are often inaccurate—especially when we do not bring the eyes of love and understanding to our perceptions, but see with the eyes of suspicion, anger, sadness, or longing. The false mode of inference is with us day after day. When we have a perception and suffer because of it, we have to ask ourselves, "Is this a true or a false inference?" Others can help us. We can ask, "I am suffering. I've had this perception, but I don't know whether it is true or false. I have heard this. I have seen this. Can you help me see whether what I have heard and seen is the truth?" When we feel angry or suspicious of others, we suffer. Rather than shut ourselves off, we should ask our friends to help. Everyone will benefit. Our suffering and our happiness are connected to the suffering and happiness of other people. We need to help each other.

With its three modes of perception, mind consciousness has access to the three fields of perception: the realm of things-in-themselves, the realm of representation, and the realm of mere images. The first field of perception, the realm of things-in-themselves, is reality as-it-is without being distorted by our ideation and mental construction. Before ideation, before the mind begins to construct, the mind touches the ultimate dimension, the realm of suchness.

The second field of perception, the realm of representation, is not reality-in-itself. It has been constructed and built by our patterns of thinking. We are used to thinking in terms of self and permanence, and we believe that things exist separately from each other. We don't see the interconnectedness, the nature of emptiness and interbeing of everything. We really believe in pairs of opposites such as birth and death, being and nonbeing, and the objects of our consciousness manifest themselves as representations, full of error. This brings us a lot of suffering.

The third field of perception is the field of mere images. We store all the images that we get from the realm of representation in our store consciousness. The image of a friend, her beauty, her anger, all these things are stored as seeds in our consciousness. We go to the archives and take these things out in order to use them. Poets and artists work a lot with this realm, combining images that already exist into new images. Dreams also occur in the realm of mere images.

Because its nature is obscured by delusion, manas is not able to touch the realm of things-in-themselves. When it is able to perceive things directly, mind consciousness is capable of touching the realm of things-in-themselves. Most of the time, however, it touches only the realms of representations and mere images. The first five consciousnesses can operate in the realm of things-in-themselves—when they are active on their own and not in combination with the discriminating function of the mind consciousness under the influence of manas. If seeing, hearing, smelling, tasting, and touching occur directly without discrimination, comparison, or a background of reminiscence, that seeing, hearing, and so on occurs in the realm of things-in-themselves. When, due to the influence of manas, the discriminating, measuring, and reasoning of the mind consciousness joins with the functioning of the first five consciousnesses, then they can only reach the realm of representations.

The realm of things-in-themselves is not distorted by false perception. The realms of representation and of mere images are. This has to do with the function of discriminating. Something is not beautiful because we like it or is ugly because we hate it. "Beautiful" and "ugly" are designations we assign to objects, based on images that arise in our mind consciousness from seeds in our store consciousness. I have been told that there are perfumes on the market called "Samsara" and "Poison." But a bottle of perfume is not samsara or poison, it is just perfume. As for being attached to perfume, liking it, hating it, or having a mental formation about it, that is our own affair. The perfume bears no responsibility for that. In France, there is a perfume called "*Je reviens*" ("I return"). When someone puts on that perfume, we identify its smell with that person. This is not something the perfume does. It is something we do, in our mind. When we are separated from the person with whom we identify that scent, it becomes a sweet mental formation. The poem, "Tale of Kieu," has the line, "The perfume makes the scent of remembering."[20] But it is not correct to place the responsibility for remembering and longing on the perfume. The responsibility lies with the seed in our consciousness and the mental formation it gives rise to. Reality-in-itself is not attached to or according to our mental formations.

That is why the Buddha said many times that dharmas (phenomena)—forms, sounds, smells, tastes, tactile objects, and objects of mind—are neither inherently wholesome nor unwholesome. It is not these things that bring pleasure, and it is not these things that are painful. It is our attachment to them that is responsible for desire and suffering. Our mind deter-

20 See the Vietnamese and English bilingual edition of Nguyen Du, *The Tale of Kieu* (New Haven, CT: Yale University Press, 1983).

mines whether or not we are caught in these things, and whether or not we are able to touch the reality of things-in-themselves. When we are feeling sad, the scenery is sad. When we are feeling joyful, the scenery is joyful. It is not the scenery itself that we find attractive or not. It is due to our own distorted perception in the realm of representation.

In our dreams, we can be sad, angry, joyful, hoping, or despairing. All the phenomena we encounter in our dreams—people, things, rivers, and mountains—belong to the realm of mere images. When we visualize a mountain during meditation, that visualization also belongs to the realm of mere images. But because this image is embraced by mindfulness, it begins to release the truth about itself and can help point to the realm of representations from which it has come. In fact, our mindful contact with the mountain may be more clear and precise than that of someone who is gazing at an actual mountain. The realm of mere images can be the door to the truth.

When we live in forgetfulness for too long, our senses and our perception become dull, and the world around us becomes unclear. We can never be happy living in such a world. Our senses and our perception need a whetstone to sharpen them, so that when we look at a flower, we can truly be in contact with the flower. That whetstone is meditation, mindfulness. There are guided meditation exercises that help sharpen our senses and bring them into contact with the wonder of life.[21]

> The realm of mere images needs only the perceiver.
> The realm of representations belongs to the lover and to the root.
> The realm of things-in-themselves, the seeds, and so forth,
> are according to the other realms.

This gatha, "The Nature of the Perceived in Itself When Not According to Our Mind," was transmitted by Xuanzang to his senior disciple, Kwaigei, who was very proficient in the Vijñaptimatrata (Manifestation Only) teachings. This verse helps us remember the functions of the three realms. The

21 See Thich Nhat Hanh, *The Blooming of a Lotus: Guided Meditation Exercises for Healing and Transformation* (Boston, MA: Beacon Press, 1993), pp. 36–43.

first line says that the realm of mere images belongs wholly to the perceiver aspect of consciousness. The realm of mere images does not have to be rooted in the realm of things-in-themselves. It is already in our mind and does not need a stimulus from the outside. Our suffering, our being tossed and turned in the realm of change, is not due to the realm of things-in-themselves but to the realm of mere images.

Remember, consciousness has two aspects: the perceiver and the perceived. The perceiver is the subject; the perceived is the object. But both subject and object are part of consciousness. "To perceive" always means to perceive *something*. Perceiving always includes both the subject and the object of perception. When we look at an oak tree, we have the tendency to think that the tree exists independent of our mind. We think that our consciousness comes out from our skull and identifies the oak tree, which is an objective reality. But the oak tree we are observing is actually an object of our consciousness. Our ideas of space and time are also objects of our perception. If we believe that the oak tree is standing outside of us in space and in time, independent of our mind, we need to look again.

Perception takes place when subject and object come together as a manifestation. It may last less than a second but in that time, both subject *and* object arise, born together at the same time. A moment after one perception has arisen, another can arise. Each perception has a subject and an object. The subject of perception is always changing and the object of perception is always changing, too.

Knowing always includes the subject who knows and the object that is known. Before we can speak about awareness, we have to ask, "awareness of what?" This is basic, but not easy to understand. Even if we think we understand something, our understanding may be limited. Please practice this diligently, and one day you will see—not merely intellectually, but in the actual experience of your life—that consciousness contains both subject and object.

The "lover" mentioned in the second line of the gatha is manas; the "root" is store consciousness. The realm of representations is a product and creation of manas, a result of its contact with the store consciousness. Seeds from the store consciousness, once they come under the influence of manas, do not remain in the realm of things-in-themselves but become part of the realm of representations. An image in the realm of representations still carries with it a small part of the realm of things-in-themselves, while an image in the realm of mere images does not.

The third line of the gatha describes how the realm of things-in-themselves and the seeds are related. It is because of other circumstances that they go with each other. Thus, the wholesome, unwholesome, and indeterminate—the "three natures" mentioned in this verse—and the seeds that the realm of things-in-themselves give rise to are linked to the three realms of perception.

The first mode of perception is direct, the second is by inference, and the third is erroneous. When perception is direct, with no discursive mentation, you reach the realm of things-in-themselves. All of us have had this kind of experience. Suppose you are deeply contemplating a beautiful, snow-covered mountain. You don't feel separate from the mountain. You are one with it in your enjoyment of it. You are the mountain, and the mountain is you. There is no subject or object. Sometimes when you contemplate the ocean you may feel that you are immense. When we touch reality with our non-thinking, nondiscriminative mode of perception, we don't make a distinction in our mind consciousness between ourselves, the perceiver, and the perceived as an "external" object of our perception. When we see in this way, we are in the realm of suchness.

There are moments like these in our lives when we can touch the ultimate dimension, but they are rare because our usual patterns of thinking do not allow for this to happen very often. Our mind tends to chop reality into pieces, and then sees each piece as existing independently from all the other pieces. That is the discriminative mind. You look at another person and think, "She is not me. Why do I have to take care of her? I have other things to do." We often discriminate like this in our everyday lives. The barrier is set up by our way of thinking. But when we learn Buddhist meditation, we try to use our intelligence to look in such a way that we can remove that kind of distinction, that kind of discrimination.

So, even the discursive, intellectual function of our mind can help us approach the ultimate dimension, if we use it to practice mindfulness. But if we do not train our mind to look deeply, no matter how much we think, reason, or speculate, our perception still belongs to the third category, false perception. The teachings use the expression *parikalpita svabhava,* which means the nature of discrimination. If this tendency to discriminate intervenes in the functioning of our mind consciousness, we always fall into the third mode of false perception, because the discriminative mind gives rise to all kinds of errors. But if we learn the Buddhist method of looking deeply, using the meditation on impermanence, nonself, and interbeing or emptiness, we begin to get away from this way of thinking and we have a chance to touch suchness. This capacity is called *nirvikalpa-jñana,* the wisdom of nondiscrimination.

Mind consciousness has access to all three modes of perception, to the three fields of perception, and it is capable of having three natures, wholesome, unwholesome, and indeterminate. When mindfulness is practiced, our mind consciousness has the capacity to be wholesome. In moments of forgetfulness, it has the capacity to be unwholesome. And it can also be indeterminate, neither wholesome nor unwholesome.

All the mental formations can manifest in mind consciousness. There are fifty-one categories of mental formations: five universal, five particular, eleven wholesome, twenty-six unwholesome, and four indeterminate. We first discussed these categories of mental formations in relation to the store consciousness in Chapter Ten; and again in relation to manas, in Chapter Twenty. First there are the five mental formations that are called universal because they operate with all eight consciousnesses. The five particular are mental formations that do not operate with every consciousness. The category of wholesome mental formations includes compassion, loving kindness, faith, and so on. The category of unwholesome mental formations includes the major afflictions such as greed, anger, and delusion, and lesser unwholesome mental states such as vexation, selfishness, envy, and so on. The indeterminate or neutral category includes four mental formations that are neither inherently wholesome nor unwholesome.[22]

Verses Twenty-Three and Twenty-Four describe the characteristics of mind consciousness that we need to understand in order to further explore its functioning in the next few verses. To sum up, mind consciousness has the widest range of contact with objects of perception (dharmas). The three

22 See Chapter 30 for a complete list of all fifty-one categories of mental formations.

modes and the three fields of perception are characteristic of mind consciousness. Mind consciousness can be of three natures (wholesome, unwholesome, or indeterminate), and it is capable of manifesting all mental formations. A perception is an act of cognition. If that act of cognition is wrong, it can create a lot of suffering and misunderstanding for the person who has it and the people around that person. That act has the mark, or nature, of unwholesomeness. When mind consciousness is capable of touching the truth, that act of cognition is called wholesome, because it has the power to liberate, to destroy ignorance in oneself and in those around us. Sometimes the act of cognition is neutral—it is not harmful, but neither has it arrived at the stage of deep looking and so it is not yet able to touch the deepest level of reality. Only with deep looking, with mindfulness, can you reveal the true nature of reality, and insight will be born. That insight leads to transformation.

25

The Gardener

Mind consciousness is the root of all actions of body and speech.
Its nature is to manifest mental formations, but its existence is not continuous.
Mind consciousness gives rise to actions that lead to ripening.
It plays the role of the gardener, sowing all the seeds.

THERE ARE THREE KINDS OF ACTION (karma)—actions of body, of speech, and of mind. Mind consciousness is the base of all three types of action. Mind consciousness directs the body to act. Whatever we say arises from mind consciousness. And it is the source of thinking, measuring, cognizing, and judging.

Like manas, mind consciousness is an evolving consciousness. However, while manas is continuous, mind consciousness is not. Sometimes mind consciousness stops operating. For example, when we sleep without dreaming, our mind consciousness stops completely. When we are in a faint, our mind consciousness may not be operating. And in the state of meditation called "no-mind," mind consciousness is also at rest. Mind consciousness is not continuous, and the same is true of the other five sense consciousnesses of eyes, ears, nose, tongue, and body. In this way, mind consciousness and the sense consciousnesses differ from the store consciousness and manas, which are continuous.

Mind consciousness gives rise to two kinds of action. One is "leading action," which draws us in one direction or another. Too often, "Mara (delusion) provides the road, and the hungry ghosts show us the direction."[23] But when the Buddha provides the road and the Sangha shows the way, it

23 In Buddhist texts, Mara is the evil one who tempts the Buddha; similar to the devil in Christianity. He is a personification of the parts of our nature that oppose our Buddha nature and prevent it from manifesting.

is beneficial for us. The second kind of action is called "ripening action." Our actions bring about the ripening of either wholesome or unwholesome seeds in our store consciousness. Mind consciousness makes both kinds of action possible—actions that propel us in a certain direction, whether for good or bad, and actions that mature the fruit of the seeds that are already present in us.

Because mind consciousness can initiate an action that leads to the ripening of seeds in our store consciousness, it is important that we learn about, train, and transform our mind consciousness. We act and speak on the basis of our thinking, our cognition. Any action of body, speech, and mind that we take based on mind consciousness, waters either positive or negative seeds within us. If we water negative seeds, the result will be suffering. If we know how to water positive seeds, there will be more understanding, love, and happiness. If mind consciousness learns to see in terms of impermanence, nonself, and interbeing, it will help the seed of enlightenment to grow and bloom like a flower.

The store consciousness is often described as the earth—the garden where the seeds that give rise to flowers and fruits are sown. The mind consciousness is the gardener, the one who sows, waters, and takes care of the earth. That is why the verse says that mind consciousness gives rise to actions leading to ripening, or maturation—the maturation of our seeds. Mind consciousness can submerge us in the hell realms or lead us to liberation, because both hell and liberation are the result of the ripening of their respective seeds. Mind consciousness does the work of initiating, and it also does the work of ripening. If it sows wheat seeds, we grow wheat.

The gardener—mind consciousness—has to trust the earth, because it is the earth that brings forth the fruit of understanding and compassion. The gardener also has to recognize and identify the positive seeds in the store consciousness, and practice day and night to water those seeds and help them grow. The garden, the store consciousness, nourishes and brings about the result. The flower of awakening, understanding, and love is a gift from the garden. The gardener only has to take good care of the garden in order for the flower to have a chance to grow.

Because the mind is the base of all actions, that is why it is so important to be mindful. Mindfulness is the best state of being for the mind. With mindfulness, our thinking and our bodily and verbal actions will go in the direction of healing and transforming. The Sangha is a great help in our practice of mindfulness. Surrounded by others who are practicing mindful speaking, mindful listening, and mindful action, we are motivated to do the same. Eventually, mindfulness becomes a habit. And with mindfulness, transformation and healing will be possible.

26

Non-Perception

Mind consciousness is always functioning
except in states of non-perception,
the two attainments,
deep sleep, and fainting or coma.

WE HAVE DISCUSSED how manas and store consciousness are continuous, always operating. Mind consciousness and the other five sense consciousnesses, on the other hand, are not continuous. There are five circumstances under which mind consciousness ceases to function. This verse describes these five circumstances: a meditative concentration (*samadhi*); the "two attainments," which are meditative states of no thinking and no perception; deep sleep; and while in a coma or in a faint.

The first condition refers to the realm of non-perception, a world in which there is no perceiving. As a human being, we can enter states of perceptionless meditation where our mind consciousness comes to a stop. But the realm of non-perception is not just a state of concentration brought about by meditation practice. When the causes and conditions are favorable, there is birth in the realm of non-perception. The realm of non-perception is seen as a higher realm, a realm with less suffering—since suffering often arises because of what we see and hear and the mental formations that arise based on our perceptions.

On our own planet, there are species of living creatures that do not have perception, that are active without perception, and perhaps they have more happiness, because mind consciousness does not function without perception. These beings also have the causes and conditions to be born in the realm of non-perception. The poet Nguyen Cong Tru writes:

In my next life, may I not be born human
but as a pine tree singing between heaven and earth.

The pine tree belongs to the realm of non-perception. This realm is much fresher than the realm of perception inhabited by human beings. If you look around, you can touch the realm of non-perception. In fact, though it may sound strange, you don't have to perceive in order to be alive. The beings that exist without perceptions are very much alive, even more joyful and healthy than we are. But human beings only understand human experience in terms of perception. When we feel unstable, agitated, afraid, or miserable, we look at the blue sky, the rocks, and the beautiful trees, and we envy them. We would like to be a beautiful tree standing on the slope of a mountain, singing in the wind.

Is it better to have perceptions or not? Much of what we see and hear every day breaks our hearts. When we are born or reborn in the world of non-perception, we live without needing mind consciousness. Manas and store consciousness continue to function in this realm. There is still the notion of a self and the energy that grasps at a self. But our eye consciousness and ear consciousness can touch the world of suchness without distorting it. With mind consciousness, we tend to distort things. So it may be a blessing to be born in the world of non-perception.

The second and third circumstances under which mind consciousness stops functioning are the "two attainments," meditations in which a state of no-mind (*achitta*) is reached. The Sanskrit word for attainment here is *samapatti*, and it refers to a kind of meditative concentration. During these two states of concentration, manas and store consciousness continue to function as usual, but they no longer receive impressions and representations.

The first of the two attainments is called the attainment of non-perception (*asamjñika samapatti*). In this state there is no perception and no need for perception. The meditator is present but does not perceive objects. His or her mind consciousness stops completely. Once, the Buddha was meditating deeply in the woods north of Vaishali. He had reached this state of non-perception and his mind consciousness had stopped functioning. On a nearby road, a large number of carts carrying merchandise passed by.

After that there was a very loud thunderstorm. But the Buddha didn't perceive any of this. When one of his disciples told him about the carts and the thunderstorm, he was surprised. He had been in the state of no-mind attainment.

The second of the two no-mind concentrations is called the attainment of cessation (*nirodha samapatti*). In this state there is no perception and no feelings, no cognition. The mind is so concentrated that it seems to be absent—every feeling, every mental formation is absent. This state is something that arhats realize.[24] It is found at the eighth stage in the career of a bodhisattva. At this stage, manas begins to let go of the store consciousness and the store consciousness is freed.

In nirodha samapatti not only mind consciousness but consciousness itself ceases to function. Here the grasping of manas begins to transform, due to the insight that the object it grasps is not self, and that subject and object are not separate but are one. We see ourselves in our universe, in other people, and in other species, and we see the universe and others in ourselves. This is called the wisdom of equality (samata jñana). It is a perception, but it is not confused or ignorant (avidya). When manas stops functioning in ignorance, store consciousness is set free of that ignorance and is very happy.

The fourth circumstance in which mind consciousness stops functioning is the state of deep sleep without dreaming. Just as some species do not have perception and yet they exist, a person who is sleeping does not perceive things, and yet is still alive. In a state of deep sleep there are no conscious dreams. When we dream, it means that our mind consciousness is active. In deep sleep, we can naturally go into the state of no-mind consciousness. Dreamless sleep is very refreshing and revitalizing because our mind consciousness, which is usually so active, is able to rest. The fifth circumstance in which mind consciousness is absent is when we fall into a faint or coma. Sometimes when we faint, our mind consciousness also stops functioning. A deep coma is a state of unconsciousness and here too the mind consciousness is not active.

24 An arhat ("worthy one") is one who has reached the state of "no more learning," has destroyed all defilements, and will not be reborn into samsara. The arhat is the highest state of spiritual attainment in Theravada Buddhism, and was the ideal of early Buddhism, in contrast to the ideal of the bodhisattva in the Mahayana.

27

States of Mind

Mind consciousness operates in five ways—
in cooperation with the five sense consciousnesses
and independent of them,
dispersed, concentrated, or unstably.

MIND CONSCIOUSNESS has five forms of action. First, it functions in cooperation with the first five sense consciousnesses of eyes, ears, nose, tongue, and body. When we see a flower, we think our perception is coming just from our eye consciousness. Sometimes that is true. But when we become *aware* of looking at the flower, our mind consciousness is also functioning. The seed of mindfulness has manifested. Mindfulness is there, and the flower is much clearer. When we look at a flower and are aware that we are looking at a flower, that is a case of mind consciousness cooperating with one of the five sense consciousnesses.

But if we look at a flower while our mind is occupied with something else, our mind consciousness is operating independently of our sense consciousness. This happens a lot in our daily lives. Suppose we are driving to work in the morning, but in our mind we are preparing for the meeting we will have later in the day. In this case, our mind consciousness is acting on its own, not in tandem with our other five sense consciousnesses. Yet we still have enough presence of mind to drive the car, even though our mind consciousness and our eye consciousness are operating independently. If a large truck suddenly turns into the road ahead of us, we manage to avoid hitting it. When we enter the parking lot, we are able to maneuver the car into a parking space. But because our mind consciousness is completely occupied, our eye consciousness has to work alone. Eye consciousness sometimes functions alone and sometimes in collaboration with mind.

Sometimes mind consciousness works alone, and sometimes it works together with one or more of the first five consciousnesses. These are the first two ways in which mind consciousness operates, with the first five consciousnesses and independent of them.When mind consciousness acts independently, as when we are dreaming, there is no coordination with the other five sense consciousnesses. We can continue to see, hear, smell, taste, and touch—but our seeing, hearing, tasting, and so on, is occurring only in the realm of mere images. We don't need our actual eyes, ears, nose, tongue, or body for this. Mere images are available to our mind consciousness from the seeds that are in our store consciousness.

We also don't need our eyes, ears, nose, tongue, or body in order to think. The mental activities of mind consciousness can operate alone. Suppose a feeling of anger arises in us that has no connection with an actual experience of one of the five sense consciousnesses—we have not stubbed our toe, for example, or observed someone doing something that we dislike, yet we feel angry. In that case, mind consciousness is operating independently. Even if we are mindful and know that we are getting angry, our mind consciousness is still operating independently. Mindfulness also can occur when the mind consciousness works in coöperation with the five sense consciousnesses or when it is operating on its own.

We can practice to become aware of the situation when our mind consciousness is working together with or independent of our first five consciousnesses. In sitting meditation, we make the effort to close the doors of our five sense gates (ayatanas) in order to concentrate our mind consciousness, to bring about an independently operating mind consciousness. When images and sounds try to invade us, we do our best not to become attached to them.

Dispersion is the third way our mind consciousness operates. In fact, it is our most frequent state of mind. We live in dispersion and forgetfulness much of the time. Our mind consciousness has the tendency to be scattered, unable to stop thinking, caught by the past and future, running in every direction. When our mind consciousness is in a state of dispersion, mindfulness is not present. We are not really alive. When we are thinking about one thing after another, when we are anxious, sad, suspicious, or imagining things, and there is no coordination of mind consciousness with the eye, ear, nose, tongue, or tactile consciousness, it is called "distracted mind consciousness." Mind consciousness is operating alone, in dispersion.

The Buddha described this type of mind consciousness as a monkey, grasping this branch and that, always changing, free-associating, jumping from thought to thought. Each of us has to recognize and embrace the monkey within ourselves with mindfulness. With mindful breathing, mindful walking, and so on, we can quiet the monkey and bring it to stillness. Mind consciousness can also be compared to a swarm of bees, buzzing around wildly and not concentrating in any one spot. Only when the queen is present will all of them gather together.

In Buddhist meditation, we practice concentration, bringing everything into sharp, clear focus. This practice is called one-pointedness of mind (*ekagrata*). The object of our concentration—the queen bee around which our swarming thoughts can gather—may be our breathing, a leaf, a pebble, a flower, or the object of our meditative focus. In the practice, we are given methods to help us concentrate the energy of our mind consciousness, to not let it become distracted. This practice is like putting a spotlight on the object of our concentration, just as when a singer or dancer is performing on stage and the spotlight is focused only on her. We focus our minds intently on the object of our concentration. When we use a lens to focus sunlight on one point, its energy is concentrated so effectively that we can burn a hole in a piece of cloth. In the same way, we focus our mind consciousness on one point in order to get a breakthrough.

Mindfulness leads us to the fourth manner of operation of mind consciousness, concentration. To solve a complex problem we have to concentrate our minds. We cannot afford to be in dispersion. With the practice of mindful breathing, we can end the state of dispersion and create a concentrated state of mind. When we use our breathing to bring all the energy of mind consciousness to one point, our confusion stops, and we are able to sustain the energy of our mind consciousness on one object. If we continue to practice, the energy of concentration will help us penetrate deeply into the heart of the object of our focus, and we will gain insight and understanding. Mind consciousness is then in a "state of concentration." The stronger and the clearer our mindfulness, the more stable our concentration. Mindfulness always brings about concentration. When we are quite concentrated, it is called "operating alone in concentration."

The fifth way that mind consciousness operates is unstably, in neurotic or psychotic states of mind. In that case, our mind consciousness is disturbed by things that have happened in the past or things that we have imagined have happened or will happen. There are conflicts between seeds in our store consciousness and conflicts between our feelings and our perceptions. When we have trouble perceiving and thinking clearly, we are said to be mentally ill. In order to heal, we have to generate whatever amount of mindfulness we can in order to begin to see things more clearly, to recognize things as they are. We may need the support of the mindfulness of our therapist, friends, and family to help us as we get in touch with the inner conflicts between our feelings and our perceptions. Practicing in this way, with the help of others, one day our mind consciousness may be freed from its instability.

Part IV

Sense Consciousnesses

Verses Twenty-Eight, Twenty-Nine, and Thirty describe the nature and characteristics of the five sense consciousnesses of eye, ear, nose, tongue, and body. We have already learned something about these five consciousnesses in our discussion of the store consciousness, manas, and mind consciousness. Just as store consciousness is the base of manas, and manas is the base of mind consciousness, these five sense consciousnesses are based in the sixth consciousness, mind consciousness. All eight consciousnesses are in this way connected and interdependent.

The senses from which these five consciousnesses arise are sometimes referred to as "gates" because all of the objects of our perception—all dharmas—enter our consciousness through sensory contact with them. For this reason, it is important to learn how to guard these gates into our consciousness, to choose wisely what we allow to enter and become seeds. The way we do this is through mindfulness.

28

Waves upon the Water

Based on mind consciousness,
the five sense consciousnesses,
separately or together with mind consciousness,
manifest like waves on water.

THE FIRST FIVE SENSE CONSCIOUSNESSES come about from the contact of a sense organ with a sense object. Eye, ear, nose, tongue, and body are the five sense organs; forms, sounds, odors, tastes, and tactile objects are the five sense objects. When our eyes see a form, eye consciousness arises, when our ears hear a sound, ear consciousness is the result, and so on. These five consciousnesses are based on the sixth consciousness, mind consciousness. They manifest either separately or together with mind consciousness like waves rising up from the ocean. Mind consciousness is like water and the five sense consciousnesses are like waves upon the water.

Sometimes a sense consciousness arises independently of the other sense consciousnesses and works only in combination with mind consciousness. Suppose we are in a gallery looking at a painting. Our attention is focused intently on the painting. Without even knowing that we have done so, we have closed off our other four sense consciousnesses. A friend may say something to us, but we do not hear him. Our ear consciousness is not functioning at that moment. Even when he puts his hand on our shoulder, we don't feel it—our body consciousness is also not functioning. All our awareness is concentrated on seeing the painting. In this example, our eye consciousness is manifesting separately, independent of the other sense consciousnesses.

When we watch television, we use both our eyes and ears. In this case, two sense consciousnesses are manifesting together. When all five sense consciousnesses are functioning at the same time, our concentration in any one of them is less strong. If we connect many lightbulbs to a single battery, each bulb will give out a weaker light. If we disconnect all but one bulb, that bulb will shine brighter. The energy of the battery, our mind consciousness, is finite. So when we concentrate our mind and focus it in one of the sense consciousnesses, the energy it can give to the task at hand will be steadier. In order to look at, hear, or smell something very clearly, our sense perception must contact the object very deeply and steadily. To do this, we allow one sense consciousness to function and close the doors of the other four sense bases. It is the same with mind consciousness; when we want to think deeply, we have to close the doors of our five sense bases in order to concentrate our mind.

When the five consciousnesses of sensation operate alone, without the intervention of mind consciousness, they are capable of touching the world of suchness, the ultimate dimension. In fact, on their own, functioning independently of mind consciousness, the five sense consciousnesses have a better chance to experience things-in-themselves than when they are operating in tandem with mind consciousness. This is because the mind consciousness, under the influence of manas, is usually caught up in cognizing and discriminating.

If eye consciousness collaborates with mind consciousness and there is no discrimination, we can also reach the realm of things-in-themselves. But mind consciousness almost always discriminates. Even if we are able to touch the world of suchness for a few seconds, we immediately lose contact with it. When mind consciousness under the influence of manas gets involved, there is processing and distortion. *Vikalpa*, the tendency to discriminate between things, to see things as this or that, as separate from and outside of one another, keeps us from staying in touch with the realm of suchness. All the objects of sensation we perceive are transformed into representations, conditioned by the seeds of delusion in our store consciousness.

That is why we must train our mind consciousness to look deeply and perceive directly. We learn about the appearance of reality—the object of perception that through our discriminating mind we turn into a representation. In Chapter Two we learned about the sign (lakshana), appearance or mark of a phenomenon. When the first five sense consciousnesses contact objects without the intervention of mind consciousness, the world of suchness, the ultimate dimension, can reveal itself. The kind of object presented in this case is called *svalakshana*, the self-mark or self-nature of the thing-in-itself. When mind consciousness intervenes, however, it generalizes everything and the self-mark of an object is transformed into a universal mark or sign (*samjña lakshana*). Things-in-themselves are transformed into representations. Our mind consciousness tends to perceive the universal marks of things. But through practice it can release the habit energy of looking at things in universal terms, and learn to touch the world of things-in-themselves directly—just as the first five sense consciousnesses can.

29

Direct Perception

Their field of perception is things-in-themselves.
Their mode of perception is direct.
Their nature can be wholesome, unwholesome, or neutral.
They operate on the sense organs and the sensation center of the brain.

THE MODE OF PERCEPTION of the five sense consciousnesses is direct (pratyaksha pramana). The sense consciousnesses do not need to operate through the medium of thought. That is why, from time to time, they are able to arrive at the realm of things-in-themselves. In this way the sense consciousnesses are like the eighth consciousness, store consciousness, which also has the direct mode of perception and whose field of perception is also the realm of things-in-themselves. Manas, the seventh consciousness, and mind consciousness, the sixth, are different. The mode of perception of manas is always false. Because of its obscuration, even when manas has a direct perception it is false. Mind consciousness is capable of all three modes of perception: direct, by inference, and false. But because it is based on and influenced by manas, its mode of perception is usually erroneous as well.

The sense consciousnesses can reach the realm of things-in-themselves in combination with mind consciousness, as long as they are functioning directly with their objects of perception. A baby looks at a toy in a way that does not use her mind very much—there is no comparison, remembering, or judging. She has not yet learned to think, "This toy is not as colorful as that toy. I like that toy better." She simply enjoys the form of the toy (the sense object) that her eyes (sense base) make contact with. That way of looking is the direct mode of perception, and through it the realm of things-in-themselves can be reached.

Once mind consciousness with its thinking and discrimination joins in, however, there is less chance for a sense consciousness to perceive the thing-in-itself. Mind consciousness tends to discriminate between things, name them, or compare them, and when it does, the realm of things-in-themselves is no longer available. The sense consciousnesses are then also operating in the realm of representations, because they arise from the mind consciousness like waves on water. Prior to the activity of mind consciousness of comparing, naming, and remembering, before seeds arise from our store consciousness and manifest as mental formations in our mind consciousness, the five sense consciousnesses are able to perceive by the direct mode. Once mind consciousness enters, it brings the seeds of memories, experiences of joy and sadness, and comparison into play, and the direct mode of perception is no longer possible.

In Chapter Twenty-Four, we learned that the Buddha said our perceptions are mostly based on memories and not on the reality of something in the present moment. When we "perceive" something we are actually remembering or comparing it with a past experience or feeling that is already present in the form of a seed in our store consciousness. Our perceptions have a great deal to do with the seeds of past experience that reside in our store consciousness. When the seeds of thinking, comparing, and judging manifest as mental formations in our mind consciousness, the image that results is not the true nature of the perceived object. Because our perception is "stained" by our emotions, memories, views, and knowledge, we cannot touch the true nature of what we observe.

When we look at a flower directly, without thinking or memories, without comparing it, whether positively or negatively, to another flower we saw a week or a year ago, we reach the realm of the flower-in-itself. This is perception "without mind." It is a function of our sense consciousness working independently of our mind consciousness, making direct contact with its object. Because it is direct, it can reach the realm of things-in-themselves. It is as innocent and fresh as a newborn baby's perception. Mind consciousness does not always function out of its experiences, sorrow, and judgments, and does not always embellish reality with them. When it doesn't, it too can reach the realm of things-in-themselves. But usually mind consciousness only reaches the realm of representations. The world we live in is heavily colored by the realm of representations. As soon as we begin to compare and discriminate (vikalpa), we are no longer contacting the object of our perception directly.

Vikalpa can also be translated as "imaginary construction." Plum Village is a reality, and when we come to Plum Village we want to know the reality of Plum Village. But because of our ideas about Plum Village, formed from what we have heard and what we ourselves have experienced in the past, we end up constructing an imaginary "Plum Village" in the realm of representations and we do not reach Plum Village-in-itself. When we are sad, it is difficult for us to be joyful even when we are looking at beautiful scenery. The landscape has been stained by our sadness. When we see someone, whether we feel happy or unhappy is mostly due to our own mind. You might see that person and feel happy, but when I see him I feel unhappy due to the unhappiness that comes from my own mind.

If we are confined within the realm of representations it is difficult to find the door into the realm of things-in-themselves. Yet we have the capacity to reach the ultimate dimension, the realm of things-in-themselves, through the direct perception of our senses. If the five sense consciousnesses are not turned upside down by the memories, sadness and joy, likes and dislikes of mind consciousness, they are able to reach the realm of things-in-themselves. By bringing the element of mindfulness into our mind consciousness we can begin to interrupt the process through which it "takes over" the sense consciousnesses. When we see or hear something, and that sight or sound evokes in us feelings of joy or sadness, mindfulness asks the question, "What is happening? Is this perception in the realm of things-in-themselves or in the realm of representations? Is this a reality outside of my own mental experience, or only an imaginary construction of my mind?" Only when we look dispassionately can we begin to see.

When operating alone, the five sense consciousnesses have a chance to touch the realm of reality. Their object is in the realm of things-in-themselves. But with the intervention of mind consciousness and its tendency to discriminate, the sense consciousnesses' capacity of direct touching is diminished. Because of this, the realm of things-in-themselves vanishes and is replaced by the realm of representations. We no longer have svalakshana, the particular. We now have samjña lakshana, the general, the universal. We have the tendency to generalize things and that is why we lose contact with the particular, which is the real thing.

The five sense consciousnesses, like mind consciousness, can also be of three natures: wholesome, unwholesome, and neutral. In the case of a direct perception touching the realm of reality-in-itself, the nature of the sense consciousnesses is wholesome. But if there is a defect in the organ, in the sense base, its mode of perception may be incorrect. In that case, its nature is either unwholesome or neutral.

In Buddhist terminology, there are two kinds of sense bases: gross and subtle. The gross sense bases are the actual organs or physical parts—the eyes, ears, nose, tongue, and body. The subtle sense bases are the nervous system associated with the sense bases, such as the optic nerve that links the eyes to the sensation center within the brain, the center of the nervous system. We see our eyes as the organs of our eye consciousness, but if we look more deeply we can also see the network of nerves behind our eyes. These are the subtle sense organs—the visual nerves, the auditory nerves, the sensation center in the brain, and so on—and they are part of the organ base for the manifestation of the sense consciousnesses.

30

Mental Formations

They arise with the
universal, particular, and wholesome,
the basic and secondary unwholesome,
and the indeterminate mental formations.

THIS VERSE describes the mental formations that go with the sense consciousnesses. We have already learned about the mental formations associated with the store consciousness (Chapter Ten), manas (Chapter Twenty), and mind consciousness (Chapter Twenty-Four). The mental formations associated with the sense consciousnesses are the five universal (*sarvatraga*), the five particular (viniyata), the eleven wholesome (*kushala*), thirteen of the twenty-six unwholesome (*akushala*), and the four indeterminate mental formations (*aniyata*).

The five universal mental formations are contact (*sparsha*), attention (*manaskara*), feeling (*vedana*), perception (*samjña*), and volition (*chetana*). All eight consciousnesses are associated with the five universal mental formations.

The five particular mental formations are zeal (chanda), determination (adhimoksa), mindfulness (smrti), concentration (samadhi), and insight (prajña). The five particular mental formations are associated with manas, mind consciousness, and the sense consciousnesses.

The eleven wholesome, or beneficial, mental formations are: faith (*shraddha*); inner shame or remorse (*hri*); outer shame or humility (*apatrapya*); absence of craving (*alobha*); lack of aversion (*advesa*); the absence of ignorance and misunderstanding (*amoha*); energy (*virya*); ease (*prasrabdhi*); carefulness (*apramada*); equanimity, nondiscrimination (*upeksa*); and nonviolence, non-harming (*ahimsa*).

The twenty-six unwholesome mental formations are: greed, craving or attachment (*raga*); aversion or hatred (*pratigha*); pride or arrogance (*mana*); ignorance or delusion (avidya); views, which here means wrong views, (*drishti*); doubt or suspicion (*vichikitsa*); anger or irritation (*krodha*); enmity or resentment (*upanaha*); hypocrisy (*mraksa*); maliciousness or spite (*pradasa*); envy or jealousy (*irsya*); selfishness (*matsariya*); deceitfulness (*maya*); guile (*sathya*); intoxication with self, mischievous exuberance (*mada*); desire to harm (*vihimsa*); lack of inner shame (*ahrikya*); lack of shame before others, lack of humility (*anapatrapya*); mental fogginess (*styana*); agitation (*auddhatya*); lack of faith, lack of confidence (*ashraddha*); indolence (*kausidya*); carelessness, negligence (*pramada*); forgetfulness, which is the opposite of mindfulness, (*mushitasmrti*); distractedness, preoccupation (*vikshepa*); and lack of recognition, lack of discernment of how things are (*asamprajanya*). The primary unwholesome mental formations are greed, hatred, and ignorance and the sense consciousnesses can be associated with these. The four indeterminate mental formations are: regret (*kaukriya*); torpor, sleepiness (*middha*); initial thought (*vitarka*); and sustained thought, investigation (*vichara*).

These are the fifty-one mental formations: the five universal, the five particular, the eleven wholesome, the twenty-six unwholesome, and the four indeterminate. When the five sense consciousnesses reach the realm of things-in-themselves through direct perception, the only concomitant mental formations they give rise to are the five universal. Mind consciousness, however, is capable of manifesting all mental formations. When the five sense consciousnesses work in tandem with the mind consciousness, they sink or swim with the mind consciousness.

PART V

The Nature of Reality

VERSES Thirty-One through Thirty-Eight discuss many of the concepts we have already learned in our study of the eight consciousnesses. Collectively, these verses explore the nature of reality. Notions of self and other, individual and collective, perceiver and perceived, birth and death, causes and conditions, are all concepts we use to understand the world we see and experience. It is important not to be caught by these concepts, and to use them only as a means to greater understanding. They are no longer needed when we reach the ultimate dimension.

The last two verses in this section, Thirty-Nine and Forty, introduce the teaching of the three self-natures (*svabhava*), the ways in which our consciousness apprehends reality. The first self-nature, *parikalpita svabhava*, is the nature of imaginary construction and discrimination. Because the mind is bound to delusion, craving, and anger, it creates false images of reality based on wrong perceptions and discrimination.

In order to unlock the door of reality, we have to observe, look deeply, and discover and put into practice the principle of the second self-nature, *paratantra svabhava. Paratantra* is the nature of interdependence. One thing can manifest only by relying on everything else. A flower can manifest based only on the requisite conditions—the rain, sunshine, soil, and other factors which make its manifestation possible.

When we are able to perceive things in the light of interdependence, one day the true nature of reality will reveal itself. This is the third self-nature, *nishpanna svabhava*, fulfilled nature or the nature of ultimate reality. The key that unlocks the door and reveals ultimate reality is paratantra, looking deeply with the eyes of interbeing.

31

Subject and Object

Consciousness always includes
subject and object.
Self and other, inside and outside,
are all creations of the conceptual mind.

THE FIRST TWO LINES of this verse are the basic teaching we need to grasp. "Consciousness," here, stands for perception and cognition. Perception and cognition are always the perception and cognition of something. There cannot be a perception that is not a perception of something.

We tend to believe that there is a knowing principle or a kind of consciousness that has an existence of its own. When we need it, we can take it out and use it. When we bring our consciousness into contact with a mountain, the consciousness knows the mountain. When it meets a cloud, it knows the cloud. Then, after letting this consciousness determine these things for us, we put it back until we need it again. This is a basic belief, but it is a misunderstanding.

It is naive to think that consciousness is something that exists independently, that it is already there and we can simply pick it up, like a garden tool, and use it to recognize an object. The Buddha said that consciousness has three parts: perceiver (subject), perceived (object), and wholeness. Subject and object work together simultaneously to manifest consciousness. There cannot be consciousness without an object. Consciousness is always consciousness of something. Thinking is always thinking of something. Anger is always being angry at someone or something. There cannot be object without subject or subject without object. Both subject and object inter-are, and they are based on wholeness.

There is nothing called "seeing" that is separate from what is seen. When our eyes contact form and color, an instant of eye consciousness is produced. But this one instant of eye consciousness does not last. If our eyes continue to be in contact with form and color, however, this flash of consciousness is repeated, moment after moment. Strung together, these instantaneous flashes form a river of eye consciousness, in which subject and object continuously support each other. This process goes on only as long as there is contact between a sense organ, in this case, our eyes, and an object.

Our sight and our eye consciousness are produced from seeds in our store consciousness. When our eyes contact form and color, they are only the conditions for development of consciousness. They alone are not enough to bring about sight or eye consciousness. There has to be a seed cause, a cause as condition (hetu-pratyaya), and this seed lies in the store consciousness. Our first seven consciousnesses—the six sense consciousnesses and manas—manifest from the eighth consciousness, the store consciousness.

When we are not mindful, mindfulness is only a seed, not a mental formation. The capacity to be mindful is available, but it is not functioning. For mindfulness to manifest it has to have an object—we are mindful of our breathing, of the person sitting in front of us, of a flower. Just as consciousness is always consciousness of something, mindfulness is always mindfulness of something. Seeing, hearing, thinking, knowing, understanding, and imagining are all consciousness, and consciousness always includes both subject and object.

In the Manifestation Only teachings, "consciousness" means the capacity to cognize, perceive, and discriminate. According to these teachings, consciousness has many different functions. So it would not be correct to say that there is one consciousness. There are as many consciousnesses as there are functions of consciousness.

When we talk about the content of consciousness, we use the term mental formations (chitta-samskara), which are psychological phenomena. We have already discussed the fifty-one categories of mental formations identified by Buddhist masters, and each contains both subject and object. Just as a river is composed of drops of water and the drops of water are the content of the river itself, so the mental formations are both the content of consciousness and consciousness itself.

The presence of a mental formation lasts only for a brief instant (*kshana*). When causes and conditions are sufficient, however, a mental formation can be regenerated as the succeeding mental formations, because mental formations can be the condition of continuity (samanantara-pratyaya). If we are showing a movie and a frame of the film has been cut out, the projector will grind to a stop at that point in the filmstrip because of the missing condition of continuity. A mental formation exists for only the shortest instant, but with favorable conditions it can be prolonged by the succession of similar mental formations, transformed by the succession of other mental formations, or regenerated.

Continuation is due to renewal and that is due to causes and conditions. If there were no renewal of the causes and conditions of something manifesting, then it would cease to manifest. Consciousness is the same. When sense base and sense object come together, consciousness comes to be. That consciousness lasts only a brief instant but because of the continuation of its causes and conditions, that consciousness arises again in the next instant and the next, the next, and the next. In this way, there is continuity of consciousness.

Until you look deeply into this process, you may think that a phenomenon is a solid, enduring entity. But after examining the way that causes and conditions continually manifest phenomena, you'll begin to see things differently. To the eyes, the glowing tip of a stick of incense quickly swirled in the darkness appears to be a constant circle of light. There is a continuity between the moment of illumination that goes before and the moment of illumination that comes after, although it is neither the same nor different. The circle of light that we make by swirling a stick of incense is really a quick succession of many points of light. Therefore, it belongs to the realm of representations. Understanding this process, we can see that it is really a series of disconnected points of light that we join together in our mind to form a circle. If we remain ignorant of this, however, we believe that we are seeing an actual circle of light.

If we look at life in this same unaware way, we may think that things are permanent and have a separate existence. With understanding, however, we see that nothing is permanent and there is nothing that exists as a separate self. Just as the circle of light is an optical illusion, our ideas of permanence and separate self are also illusions of perception and cognition. When we look deeply enough we can see that all material and psychological phenomena are evolving and changing in every moment. Then we see the substance of reality, and our insight into impermanence and nonself will prevent us from being caught in illusion.

The fifth century B.C.E. Greek philosopher Heraclitus reached a similar conclusion when he observed that the water of the river he had swum in five minutes earlier was not the same water he was standing in five minutes later. "We can never step into the same river twice," he said. Heraclitus' observation was an insight into impermanence and nonself, although he did not use those terms.

All phenomena—physical, physiological, and psychological—manifest and transform this way. When causes and conditions are sufficient, a phenomenon is produced for an instant; as these causes and conditions repeat themselves, the phenomenon is again produced. This steady stream of production gives the illusion of permanence, but in fact each phenomenon that is produced is new. The phenomenon of one instant dies and a new phenomenon is born in the next instant.

Self and other, inside and outside, are concepts. Concepts are produced by our consciousness. Using the sword of concepts, we cut reality into pieces and create boundaries between things. From the point of view of ordinary perception, things exist independent of one another. We see the cloud existing outside of the rose. But using the keys of impermanence and nonself, we can open the door of reality and see that the cloud does not lie outside the rose, nor does the rose lie outside the cloud. If there is no cloud, there is no rain; if there is no rain, there is no water; if there is no water, there is no rose. As the rose decomposes, the water in it evaporates and returns to the cloud. Looking deeply this way, our concepts about boundaries disappear and we can see the cloud in the rose, the rose in the cloud.

The teachings of this verse have the flavor of the Avatamsaka Sutra, which says, "The one is in the all, and the all is in the one." One thing contains everything else. In the everything is the one. In our own age, atomic physicists who have looked deeply into the molecular world have had to abandon concepts of inside and outside, self and other. They know that one atom is made up of all other atoms. One electron is made up of all other electrons. In a molecule or an atom, we can see the presence of all other molecules and atoms. One atom contains the whole universe. In one person, everything in the universe is present. I am in you, and you are in me. This is, because that is. This is not, because that is not. The teachings of Interdependent Co-Arising (pratitya-samutpada), when developed to their highest level, become the teaching of infinite layers of causes and conditions.[25] One is all, and all is one.

I know that you are still there
because I am still here.
The arms of perception embrace all,
joining life to death, subject to object, everything to everything else.

When I taught the Manifestation Only teachings at Van Hanh Buddhist University in Vietnam in the mid-1960s, I often recited this poem at the end of the course. It helped the students understand these teachings. But without a basic grasp of the fundamental teachings of Manifestation Only, this poem may seem impossible to understand.

A Vietnamese Zen master of the Ly dynasty (11th century C.E.) said, "If the smallest grain of sand exists, everything exists. If the smallest grain of sand does not exist, then nothing else exists." Only one grain of sand needs to exist for everything else to exist. Another master of the same era said, "The whole Earth can be placed at the tip of a hair. The sun and the moon can fit in a mustard seed."[26]

Our sword of conceptualizing, our discriminating mind, separates things into self and other, inside and outside. We think that consciousness is inside and the object of consciousness is outside. But the notion of outside exists only because we have the notion of inside. Inside of what? To say mind consciousness exists inside our body is not true. To say it exists outside our body is also not true.

25 For an in-depth discussion of Interdependent Co-Arising, see Thich Nhat Hanh, *The Heart of the Buddha's Teaching*, Chapter 27.
26 Master Khanh Hy (1067–1142).

In the Shurangama Sutra, the Buddha demonstrated that consciousness is neither inside, outside, or in the middle.[27] The Diamond Sutra presents the concepts of self, human being, living being, and lifespan for us so that we may transcend them.[28] These teachings help us remove our concepts and they are part of our study of the Manifestation Only teachings.

When we go beyond concepts, we begin to understand these teachings. But if we believe that there is *only* consciousness and that outside of consciousness nothing exists, we are still caught in the concepts of inside and outside and are not practicing according to the teachings. The teachings are designed to help us go beyond *all* concepts, including the concepts of "consciousness" and "Manifestation Only."

The notion of self relies on the notion of nonself. Both ideas are products of our conceptual mind. Reality is free from notions. In Buddhism, nonself is a crucial teaching, an instrument to help us explore reality, to help us liberate ourselves. It is an antidote for "self." We need it because we cling to our self and are victims of the notion of self. But the teaching is not something to worship. Self is a product of the mind. Nonself is also a product of the mind. When we are able to touch reality, both notions will be removed. When we are ill, we need medicine to neutralize the illness. Once we have recovered, the medicine is no longer needed.

While studying this book, you may arrive at some insight concerning Manifestation Only. If you realize the importance of going beyond concepts such as birth and death, self and other, inside and outside, you will be liberated from the desire to use reason to prove your understanding. When people ask you about "Manifestation Only" or consciousness you will not have to explain anything to them. You can just smile. If someone asks you, "Is consciousness one or many?" say that consciousness is neither one nor many. Only when you have awakened understanding will your words have value.

Consciousness always includes subject and object of consciousness. Self and other, inside and outside are all creations of our conceptual minds.

27 See the Shurangama Samadhi Sutra, translated by John McRae (Berkeley, CA: Numata Center, 1998).

28 See Thich Nhat Hanh, *The Diamond That Cuts through Illusion: Commentaries on the Prajñaparamita Diamond Sutra* (Berkeley, CA: Parallax Press, 1992).

This has been transmitted to us by many generations, and is called twofold or double grasping. First is the grasping of the subject of perception as self, and second is the grasping of the object of perception as an external, objective reality. In fact, both subject and object belong to perception. We have to train our minds in order to be able to release both kinds of grasping.

Concepts like self and other, inside and outside, are the result of double grasping. In Buddhist practice, not only is low self-esteem an illness, but high self-esteem is also an illness, and thinking that you are the equal to someone else is an illness as well. Why? Because all three of these ideas are based on the notion that you are separate from the other. Understanding interbeing can cure this illness and establish perfect harmony between so-called self and so-called other.

Fritz Perls, one of the founders of the Gestalt school of therapy, has often been quoted as saying: "I do my thing, you do your thing; I'm not here in this world to live up to your expectations.... You are you, and I am I, and if by chance we find each other, it's beautiful; if not, it cannot be helped." This statement is on the notion of self and other as separate entities. It is not based on the insight of interbeing. I am not very fond of this statement. At the very least I expect you to take care of yourself, because if you take good care of yourself, I will suffer less. My students have the right to expect me to be a good teacher. This means I must practice what I teach—that is only fair. And I have the right to expect my students to put into practice what they have learned from me. That, too, is only fair.

I would like to offer this gatha as a response to the statement of Mr. Perls:

You are me and I am you.
Is it not true that we inter-are?
You cultivate the flower in you so that I will be beautiful,
And I transform the garbage in me so that you don't have to suffer.

This is the kind of insight that is based on interbeing. If we live our lives according to this insight, we will not have to suffer so much.

32

Perceiver, Perceived, and Wholeness

Consciousness has three parts—
perceiver, perceived, and wholeness.
All seeds and mental formations
are the same.

THIS VERSE IS A SNAKE. If you are not careful, you will be bitten by it. Reading it, you may think it teaches that consciousness has three parts. But this verse is intended only as a skillful means to show us something. Don't get caught by the idea that consciousness is something that can be divided into three separate parts. The divisions are only a framework designed to help us understand the reality of consciousness. Once we understand, we can stop dividing. Suppose I draw a circle and I divide it in two by a vertical line. The circle is the base—consciousness—and from that base are manifested the subject and the object of consciousness. But these two halves never leave the whole of the circle, just as waves never leave the water. If you think that any one part exists separately from the other parts, you have been bitten by the snake.

When I was studying the Manifestation Only teachings as a young monk, my teacher illustrated this verse by drawing a picture of a snail crawling over a leaf. He designated the two antennae of the snail as perceiver and perceived, and the body of the snail as the base, the thing-in-itself. The first antenna represents the subject of perception, the second one the object of perception, and the entire body of the snail represents the base of both and the whole substance of perception. My teacher once picked up a snail from a bush to show me. When you touch a snail's antennae, it pulls them in. Likewise, the perceiver and perceived aspects of consciousness may not always appear. Perception then returns to its base, where you cannot see its two aspects: subject and object.

Consciousness has three parts: perceiver, perceived, and wholeness. The subject (*darshana-bhaga*) is the first aspect of perception. The second is the object of perception (*nimitta-bhaga*). The third aspect, the base of both subject and object, is wholeness (*svabhava-bhaga*). Subject and object are born at the same time. When the snail sends up its antennae, he sends up both at the same time. Consciousness can manifest or fail to manifest, depending on whether both the perceiver and the perceived aspects manifest. When consciousness manifests, we say it exists. When it does not manifest, we say it does not exist. But this idea of existing and not existing causes us to suffer. The subject of perception manifests at the very moment that the object of perception manifests, and neither is possible without the base. Wholeness is everything.

This is true for the eight consciousnesses, and for each seed and mental formation as well. All seeds and mental formations also have these three elements—subject, object, and base—because they all belong to consciousness. Every mental formation, every object of perception, every seed within our consciousness has these three aspects and these aspects cannot be separated from one another. They can only coexist. Lacking any one, the other two cannot be.

The teachings of the Avatamsaka Sutra tell us that the infinitely small contains the infinitely large and the infinitely large contains the infinitely small. If that is so, then the infinitely small has the same nature as the infinitely large. An atom, a leaf, or a trail of vapor each carries within it all the information needed to understand the entire cosmos. When we discover the truth of an atom, we discover the truth of the whole universe. When we understand a single drop of water in the ocean, we understand the whole ocean. If we look deeply enough into a pebble we can see the universe.

Looking into a leaf, we see the sun and the clouds. Looking into our bodies, we see the whole universe and everything that exists in the universe. Looking into just one thing deeply, we understand all things. Noumena and phenomena, the ultimate and historical dimensions, always go together. They are not two distinct entities. Each cell of our body contains all our ancestors and all future generations. Each seed, mental formation, and consciousness in us contains the whole cosmos, all of time and all of space. You don't have to go on a long journey to discover this. You don't have to meditate on many subjects to obtain this insight. If you can perceive deeply the true nature of any mental formation, whether wholesome or unwholesome, you can reach full enlightenment. Just shed light on one thing, and you can understand all that exists.

In the one, you can identify the all. The seed of anger in you, even before it manifests as a mental formation, possesses all three parts within itself. The seed of anger also touches all of your other seeds—including seeds of love and reconciliation. How is it that love is contained within anger, and anger is contained within love? Just as a flower is made of non-flower elements, anger is made of non-anger elements. The one contains the all. But because of our tendency to think in terms of discrimination, we think that our seeds of love and anger are separate.

Each teaching of the Buddha contains all his other teachings. If we look deeply into the First Noble Truth—the truth of the existence of suffering—we see the other three noble truths: the cause of suffering, the possibility of release from suffering, and the way to free ourselves from suffering. Looking deeply into suffering, we see the way out of suffering. Interbeing—the one contains the all—is a very important aspect of the Buddha's teaching, perhaps the most important teaching to help us free ourselves from suffering. We don't need to learn everything. If we learn one thing deeply, we can understand all the teachings. We need to train ourselves to look in this way.

Each of our afflictions, our unwholesome mental formations, contains Buddha nature and liberation. Our anger includes all the factors that brought it about. If our anger did not contain liberation, how could we transform it into non-anger? In our compost are many fragrant flowers. A skillful gardener does not get rid of kitchen garbage but turns it into compost. In the course of time, the garbage will turn into a basket of fresh, green vegetables. If we know how to compost our afflictions of greed, hatred, ignorance, pride, doubt, views, agitation, torpor, and forgetfulness, we can transform them into peace, joy, liberation, and happiness.

There is no need to push anything out of existence. In fact, there isn't anything we can push out of existence. If we could push one thing out, we would have to push everything out, because the one contains the all. When we come into the kitchen on a winter day, we feel warm and comfortable.

Our feeling of warmth and comfort is not only due to the stove in the kitchen, but to the coldness outside. If the weather outside wasn't cold, we wouldn't have the feeling of comfort when we enter the warm kitchen. Pleasant feelings are made by unpleasant feelings. Unpleasant feelings are made by pleasant feelings. This is, because that is. One mental formation contains all other mental formations. Every seed contains all other seeds. The seed of anger contains within itself the seed of love. The seed of delusion contains within itself the seed of enlightenment. Each gene in our own cells contains all other genes. In a good environment, an unhealthy gene can slowly turn into a healthy gene. This insight can open up many doors of modern therapies. This is the teaching of the Buddha. When we forget this, we drift in the world of birth and death. But when we transform our forgetfulness into mindfulness, we see that there is nothing we need to reject or discard.

33

Birth and Death

Birth and death depend on conditions.
Consciousness is by nature a discriminatory manifestation.
Perceiver and perceived depend on each other
as subject and object of perception.

According to the Manifestation Only teachings, "birth" simply means manifestation, the appearance of a phenomenon. "Death" means the absence of manifestation or appearance. Birth and death come about based on conditions. When conditions are favorable, there is birth (manifestation) and there is death (the absence of manifestation).

When we look deeply and recognize the causes and conditions that allow birth and death to be, we realize that birth and death are only notions. The manifestation of something is not the beginning of its existence, and when something is not manifesting, this does not mean that it does not exist. Before a phenomenon manifests, it is already there in the conditions. Birth is made of death, and death is made of birth. Birth and death occur simultaneously in each moment. Before you were born, you were already there. When you die, you do not become nothing. You go back to the wholeness, to the base, in order to manifest again.

Everything that is manifested has to rely on conditions. If conditions are sufficient, then manifestation is perceived. If conditions are not sufficient, we do not perceive the manifestation. Unmanifested is not the same as non-existent. When the snail has retracted its antennae, it would not be correct to say the antennae do not exist. After we walk away and the snail puts out its antennae again, it would not be correct to say that they have only at that moment come into existence.

In the same way, when consciousness manifests, it is not, at that moment, born. When it does not manifest, it does not, at that moment, die. When consciousness manifests, there is differentiation and discrimination (vikalpa). Discrimination says, "This is self, and that is other than self." It is the sword that cuts and divides what is self from what is not self. But discrimination is not the truth. It is an imaginary construction, a fabrication of the mind. The Chinese ideogram for the term vikalpa means "universal comparing." To compare is to say, "This is inside, but that is outside. This continues to exist, but that ceases to exist."

The perceiver and the perceived—two of the three aspects, or faces, of consciousness—depend on each other in order to manifest. Neither can exist independently. When you are angry, there is always an object of your anger—you are angry with someone or at something. When you are in love, you are in love with someone. If you are jealous, your jealousy has an object. Sometimes we say of a jealous person, "He is jealous of a shadow," or "She is jealous of the wind." Even if the object of your jealousy has no reality, a mere shadow of the wind, "shadow" and "wind" are objects nonetheless.

When a woman learns that she is pregnant, she already begins to love the baby. She visualizes the baby growing in her womb, what it will look like, its sweet smile, and she is sure that this image of her baby belongs to the realm of things-in-themselves. But the object of her love still belongs to the realm of mere images; it is really an imaginary construction. The mind differentiates and compares in order to develop this image. That is why the verse says that consciousness is by nature a discriminatory manifestation.

The nature of consciousness is to manifest perception in which subject and object support each other to make the perceiver and the perceived possible. Consciousness manifests as rivers, mountains, stars, and sky. When we look at the rivers, mountains, stars, and sky, we can see thinking in the deep blue waters and perception in the stars. This is true because all these phenomena are manifestations of consciousness, objects of perception, both collective and individual. What we believe to be an objective reality is first of all the object of our perception.

We have to distinguish between the words "consciousness" and "manifestation." For consciousness, we use the Sanskrit word "vijñana." But the word used by Vasubandhu, the author of the *Thirty Verses*, is "vijñapti", which means to manifest, to inform, to give information. The Sanskrit prefix "*vi-*" means to distinguish, discern, analyze, understand, or cognize. When something has not yet manifested, we call it *avijñapti*.

If I show you my hand, you cannot see my ability to do calligraphy, but that doesn't mean that this capacity does not exist. It is simply avijñapti, unmanifested. If I were to take a piece of paper and a brush and make some movement with my hand, you would then see its capacity to do calligraphy. It would then be vijñapti, manifested. A manifestation means that both a subject of perception and, at the same time, an object of perception have manifested.

Birth and death depend on conditions. Production and disintegration depend on conditions. Consciousness does not manifest only as the subject of perception, the perceiver. When there is manifestation of consciousness, it is, at the same time, both aspects of perception—perceiver and perceived.

34

Continuous Manifestation

In individual and collective manifestation,
self and nonself are not two.
The cycle of birth and death is achieved in every moment.
Consciousness evolves in the ocean of birth and death.

WHEN WE LOOK into any phenomenon—material, physiological, or psychological—we can see how much individuality and how much collectivity is in it. We may think of Plum Village as completely objective. The Upper Hamlet is two miles from the Lower Hamlet, and distance is certainly an objective phenomenon. But each of us has our own experience of the distance between the two hamlets. For some people, the walk from the Upper to the Lower Hamlet is very short; for others it seems very long. Everyone who lives in Plum Village has a unique image of Plum Village. In each case, the amount of individual manifestation exceeds the amount of collective manifestation. But there is also an element of collectivity in these images; they have certain things in common. We need to practice looking deeply in order to see how much individuality and how much collectivity there are in the objects of our perception.

We also need to ask, When there is a collective manifestation, whose manifestation is it? A table is made of wood. It is something stable and I can put a teacup on it. The image of a table as furniture is a collective one, shared by other human beings. But a wood worm does not share in this collective manifestation. Instead, the worm sees the table as a huge banquet that will last for many months. The image of an object of perception depends on the seeds that arise from the store consciousness of the perceiver. No manifestation is wholly individual or wholly collective.

The seeds of anger in us are our individual manifestation, because they cause us to suffer. But this doesn't mean that they have nothing to do with others. When we are angry it is difficult for those around us to be happy. In this way, our anger is also a collective manifestation. All phenomena are individual and collective at the same time. Just as a hole in the ozone layer is linked to the survival of all species on Earth, the happiness or suffering of someone living in Cambodia is linked to the happiness or suffering of someone living in North America. When we can see into the essence of collective and individual manifestation, ideas of self and other, self and nonself will cease to exist.

In the beginning, we distinguish between self and nonself, me and you, and we are concerned only with what has to do with ourselves. But, after awhile we discover that if we do not look after what is not ourselves, the consequences will be dire. If we do not take good care of our partner, we will receive the effects of our non-caring. If we do not demonstrate our concern about the hole in the ozone layer, we will suffer the consequences of our lack of concern.

For centuries, the nations referred to as developed have behaved selfishly, looking after only their own "national interest." They only care about their own economies, their own cultures, and the education of their own people. They say that it is not their business to take care of other countries. But if so-called developed countries do not acknowledge their responsibility to the so-called Third World, the developed countries will also die.

According to the teachings of Interdependent Co-Arising, the life of developed countries depends on the life of underdeveloped countries. When technology is developed, many commodities are produced and there has to be a market to sell them to. In the initial search for markets and supplies of natural resources to fuel their own economies, more developed nations undertake warlike expeditions in order to claim territories. Over time, however, the colonizers have had to let go of their colonies. Nowadays, the industrialized nations use diplomacy and offer technological and economic aid. But their motivation is not really altruistic. Their interest in other countries is still self-serving: by helping develop a new country they hope that it will become a market for its commodities. "Third World" countries borrow money in order to develop their economies but often they cannot develop fast enough, go bankrupt, and cannot repay the loan. If the international currency system collapses, the ramifications will reach back into the developed countries and they will also suffer. Nations are beginning to learn the lesson of interbeing.

At first, we establish self and what is not self. Slowly we learn that the self we have established does not exist as something separate, because it is completely dependent on what is not self. So then we have the idea of nonself. Using the idea of nonself, we are able to go beyond the idea of self. But the idea of nonself is also dangerous. If we go beyond the idea of self only to be caught in the idea of nonself, we are no better off. Nonself as an idea is also a prison. In the Discourse on the Dharma Seal, we learn that nirvana is going beyond *all* ideas, not only ideas of permanence and self but also ideas of impermanence and nonself. The teaching of nonself is designed to save us from the idea of self. But if we hold on to nonself as a concept, an idea, in which to take refuge, we are just as much imprisoned by it as we were before by the idea of self. We have to go beyond all concepts.

Many Buddhists (and non-Buddhists) talk about nonself in a way that shows that they are still caught in ideas. Their talk about nonself does not lessen their idea of self in the slightest. Even though they endlessly discuss the teachings of nonself, they have not been helped by them. They are still imprisoned in ideas, and they continue to suffer in their everyday lives. To free themselves they must put an end to the idea of nonself as well as to the idea of self, and see that self and nonself inter-are. The teaching of nonself is possible only because there is the idea of self. Self and nonself are not two.

When we look deeply into collective and individual manifestation, we see that self and nonself cannot be separated from each other. We also see that the cycle of rebirth recurs in every instant. We do not have to wait until we die to be reborn. We are being reborn in every moment. Think back to the circle of light made by the stick of incense: that light is reborn in each instant. The light of this moment is the rebirth of the light of the previous moment. Nor is it true that we have another ten or twenty or fifty more years until we die. In fact we are dying in every moment. We are dying right now and our death could bring about something very beautiful and precious, just as the death of one instant of light makes it possible for the next instant of light to be reborn.

Usually we think it takes eighty or a hundred years to complete one cycle of birth and death. But we can experience birth and death in every moment, within our body and within our consciousness. Cells of our body die every moment in order to make room for other cells. If we organize a funeral every time a cell dies, we would spend all our time mourning and not have any time left to do other things. If we see that it is necessary for our body—our cells—to die, so that new cells can be born, we will not spend time bemoaning our loss. It would be a shame to view this process as a sorrowful thing. The cycle of rebirth relies on the paths of body, speech, and mind. In every instant we have to communicate the energy of lightness, liberation, peace, and joy so that life, the cycle of birth and death, can be more beautiful for us and for everyone.

Rebirth is neither a straight nor a winding path. We may have the idea that rebirth is a straight path that has already been determined—the you of this moment will become the you of the next moment, and so on. But it is not that simple. Many winding paths make up the cycle of rebirth. In every instant, we are receiving input from the universe, society, our food, our education, our loves, and our hates. At the same time, we are producing output, breathing out carbon dioxide, making other people happy or sad. To say that we are going on a straight path in a certain direction is not correct. In every instant, we go out into all directions.

Fifty years ago I wrote a book on the basic teachings of the Buddha. Can we trace the path of that book? Many people who read that book have already died, but their children, grandchildren, and great-grandchildren have received ideas from it. We cannot follow the path of that book in one direction only. Nor can we see all the directions in which the author has gone. Each time we say or do something, write a line of poetry, disseminate an idea, send a letter, we go out in many different directions. Once we have set out in these directions, there is no way we can pull ourselves back to the place we were before.

We think that when we arrive at a certain point we die, but that is not the way it is. We are already present in all corners of the universe. What is it that dies? The dead body is just our insignificant remains. We are already in all corners of the universe. We are present in our children, students, friends, readers—all the people we have made happy and all the people we have made suffer. We are in a cycle of rebirth in every instant. To say that it is only when we arrive at a certain point that we die and begin to enter the cycle of rebirth, is oversimplified. Everything possesses the nature of interbeing within itself. The cycle of birth and death is achieved in every moment. Self and nonself are not two distinctive entities; they are not separate. Once we have touched deeply the nature of interbeing, we will not separate self and nonself.

All eight consciousnesses, all the seeds, and all the mental formations together with their objects, including our body, are evolving in the ocean of birth and death. Always evolving, always flowing, collective or individual, store consciousness is like a river. Our sense consciousnesses are like rivers. Birth and death are happening in each of these rivers, and these rivers are traversing the cycle of rebirth in every instant. When we understand this and our understanding expresses itself in our life, we reach the state of non-fear. If we see it only as a theory, it will not bring us to the state of fearlessness. The state of non-fear is the state of no birth and no death, of not many and not one. Without this living insight, we will remain in fear.

Birth means manifestation and death means non-manifestation. A non-manifestation and a new manifestation can take place simultaneously. The ending of a cloud and the beginning of the rain can be seen as simultaneous. In fact, there is nothing ending and nothing beginning. There is only a flow of manifestation. Non-manifestation can also be understood as a manifestation. Manifestation and cessation of manifestation are taking place in every moment. If you look at the separate frames of a motion picture film, you see only static images. But if you run the film through a projector, you see the dynamic flow of life, and you have the impression that there is no beginning and ending, no birth and no death. In fact, birth and death are taking place every moment. We are floating on the ocean of birth and death right now. When we are able to see the cycle clearly with our insight and wisdom, we no longer need to be afraid of it. We will know how to enjoy floating on the ocean of birth and death.

We should not postpone reflecting on or meditating about death. We must learn to die in every moment in order to enjoy being reborn again and again. We have to train ourselves to see birth and death only as manifestations. Birth is a continuation, and death is also a continuation in other forms. The death of the cloud also means the birth of rain. The nature of the cloud and the rain are really the nature of no-birth and no-death, the nature of continuation, the nature of continuous manifestation.

35

Consciousness

Space, time, and the four great elements
are all manifestations of consciousness.
In the process of interbeing and interpenetration,
our store consciousness ripens in every moment.

EVERY DHARMA, every phenomenon, is conditioned. Conditioned dharmas are combinations of other elements. A flower, for example, is made of the elements of clouds, sunshine, seeds, minerals, and so on. In the past, Buddhist masters taught that there are some dharmas that are not conditioned. They said that space is not conditioned by anything, and so it is an "unconditioned dharma." But we know that just as a flower is made of non-flower elements, space is also made of non-space elements, so it too is a conditioned dharma.

"The four great elements" are earth, water, fire, and air. They are the four energies of the material universe. Earth is the energy of solidity. Water is fluid and penetrating. Fire is heat and warmth. Air is the force that leads to movement. These four energies can be transformed into other energies. A waterfall can become electricity and therefore light. We should not think of these four elements as separate or independent. They depend on one another. Sometimes space and consciousness are added to these four fundamental elements to make six elements. Sometimes time and direction bring the list to eight. All the elements, including space and time, are manifestations of consciousness.

We usually think of space as something empty. But physicists have shown that when matter is diluted, it becomes space. The theory of relativity shows that space and matter are one reality. If there is no space, there is no matter. If there is no matter, there is no space. Space—a seemingly empty phenomenon—is able to bend matter, a seemingly solid phenomenon. We look at a galaxy and it appears curved. If you put a branch in a glass vase filled with water, the branch will look as though it is curved, or broken.

Time is also energy. Time makes space, and space makes time. Outside of time, there can be no space. Outside of space, there can be no time. Einstein has said clearly that space and time are two aspects of the same reality.

> Let us go together to climb the nameless mountain,
> let us sit on the ageless blue-green stone,
> quietly watching time weave the silken thread
> that creates the dimension called space.[29]

Space is one aspect of a manifestation of reality. Another aspect is time. We may first see a manifested reality as space, but later it may be seen as time. We think that such a phenomenon as winter belongs to time. In North America, the month of January is considered winter. But if we travel to Australia in January, we find that it is summer there. The Big Bang and the expansion of the cosmos can only be conceived of in terms of space and time. We can see time because we can touch the expansion of the cosmos. We can see the expansion of the cosmos only because we can touch time. Time and space are aspects of the same reality, a reality that manifests itself sometimes as time and sometimes as space. Time and space inter-are. We cannot separate one from the other. Both are manifestations of consciousness.

Consciousness manifests in many forms. Consciousness is an energy that helps form earth, water, fire, and air, the four great elements. Each of the elements contains all the others. We cannot separate reality into pieces and say that this piece is not that piece. We know that this piece includes all the other pieces. One energy includes another, like the waterfall that gives energy to produce electric light. Our body is an energy and so is our thinking. Each energy influences all the others. This is interbeing.

29 See Thich Nhat Hanh, "True Source," in *Call Me by My True Names: The Collected Poems of Thich Nhat Hanh* (Berkeley, CA: Parallax Press, 1999), p. 116.

In Western logic, the "principle of identity" says that A is only A, and not B. A flower can only be a flower. It cannot be a cloud. But this principle is based on the notion that things are permanent and have a separate self. Buddhism begins by using the idea of nonself to help us look deeply into the nature of things. Nonself is an aspect of impermanence. Although impermanence is usually understood in terms of time and nonself in terms of space, in fact time and space are one, and nonself and impermanence are also one. The only clear way to contemplate nonself is in the light of interbeing. Interbeing recognizes that A is B, that this is also that.

Recall physicist David Bohm's description of the "explicate order" and the "implicate order." In the explicate order, we see things as existing outside of and separate from all other things. In the implicate order, we see that all things lie within other things. In the world of microscopic particles, one particle is made of all other particles. Modern physicists are beginning to understand reality much in the way of the Avatamsaka Sutra.

Interbeing and interpenetration are ripening all the time. Ripening, or maturation (vipaka) means the combination of many elements that bring about a result. To make soup we put different ingredients into a pot, apply heat, and wait. After a while, the combination of elements becomes something delicious that we can eat. Maturation does not take place only once every one hundred years. Maturation takes place in every moment. The maturation of store consciousness takes place in every moment. Every day we are born again.

Store consciousness ripens in two ways—as our person and as our environment. In this moment, we can touch the ripened fruit that is ourself, our friends, and our world. Tomorrow, that ripened fruit will be different—better or worse, depending on our individual and collective actions. In Buddhism, action (karma) takes three forms: actions of body, speech, and mind. When our actions of body, speech, and mind are brought together, they create the qualities of our happiness or suffering. We are the author of our destiny. The quality of our being depends upon the quality of our prior actions. This is called maturation.

Some seeds take longer to ripen than others. Some maintain the same basic nature before and after ripening. Some are completely different before and after ripening. Someone could sow a musical seed. Before that seed ripens, we do not sing well and the melodies we compose are not very beautiful. As we practice more and more, the seed ripens and there is a change and the music we create becomes more melodious. Ripening takes place in every moment. Our body, our consciousness, and the world are the matured fruits of this ripening.

Consciousness is at the heart of everything. Space, time, and the four great elements are all displays of consciousness. All have the nature of interbeing; if we look deeply into one, we find the other five. Looking into space, we see time and the other elements as well.

We have the power to create and arrive at a new maturation when we know how to transform the seeds in our store consciousness. We may think that a new maturation takes place only after we release this body, this actual manifestation of our eight consciousnesses. But looking deeply, we see that maturation takes place in every moment. We have the capacity to renew ourselves in every moment.

36

No Coming, No Going

Beings manifest when conditions are sufficient.
When conditions lack, they no longer appear.
Still, there is no coming, no going,
no being, and no nonbeing.

"CONDITIONS" here refers to causes and conditions. We first learned about causes and conditions in Chapter Eighteen. The Manifestation Only school of Buddhism lists four kinds of conditions that help things manifest. The base or foundation cause is called the seed cause, or cause as condition (hetu-pratyaya). Then there are the condition for development (adhipati-pratyaya), object as condition (alambana-pratyaya), and the condition of immediate continuity (samanantara-pratyaya).

In truth, things do not begin to exist. The birth of a baby isn't the beginning of his existence. He has been there all the time; only now does he begin to manifest in that form. A piece of paper, before it manifests, already existed in the clouds and the trees. If we were to burn it, it would not cease to exist. The smoke would go into the clouds, and the warmth will go into the atmosphere. These things do not depart. They either manifest or are latent.

When conditions are sufficient, a phenomenon (dharma) manifests. When causes and conditions are lacking, it does not manifest. When we begin to be angry, it does not mean that the anger is just at that moment coming into being. The anger was already there as a seed in our store consciousness. Then, when someone does something that annoys us and the seed of anger ripens, our face turns red, our voice rises or becomes unsteady, and other outward signs of anger arise. But it would not be correct to say that our anger only at that moment began to exist—anger was already present as a potential in our consciousness.

The same is true of our body and mind. The body manifests when conditions are sufficient. When the conditions are no longer sufficient, the body ceases to manifest. It has not come from anywhere and it will not go anywhere. This is the teaching of no coming, no going. Where have I come from? Where will I go after I die? These are misleading questions. When conditions are sufficient, the body manifests. When conditions are no longer sufficient, the body returns to latency. If we look deeply, we can remove the notions of coming and going.

We need to go beyond ideas of being and nonbeing, coming and going, same and different, birth and death. Coming into existence and going out of existence are only a pair of opposites. In reality, there is no coming and no going. The Buddha is described as someone who has come from suchness and goes to suchness, which means reality as it is. Suchness is not something that can be described as here or there, coming or going. Coming from suchness means coming from nowhere. Going to suchness means going nowhere. There is truly no coming, no going, no being, and no nonbeing. Being and nonbeing are merely mental categories we use to grasp reality. Reality is free of these notions. The true nature of reality is nirvana, freedom from notions. Everything goes beyond these dualities.

When someone you love passes away, do not look for that person in space or time. When conditions are no longer sufficient, the body returns to latency. If we look deeply, we can remove the notions of coming and going.

There are four pairs of ideas we need to go beyond: being and nonbeing, coming and going, same and different, birth and death. Coming into existence and going out of existence are only a pair of opposites. In reality, there is no coming and no going. The Buddha is described as the Tathagata, someone who has come from suchness and goes to suchness. Suchness means reality as it is. Suchness is not something that can be described as here or there, coming or going. Coming from suchness means coming from nowhere. Going to suchness means going nowhere. There is truly no coming, no going, no being, and no nonbeing. Being and nonbeing are merely mental categories we use to grasp reality. Reality is free of these notions.

The true nature of reality is nirvana—freedom from notions. Everything goes beyond these dualities—the Buddha, you, the leaf, the mango. As far as reality is concerned, these ideas do not apply.

Through the teachings of Interdependent Co-Arising, we can go beyond ideas of existence and nonexistence. If only one cause or condition is lacking, that which is to manifest will remain latent. When you come to Plum Village in July, there are many fields of sunflowers, and you say that the sunflowers exist. But if you were to come in April, you would not see any sunflowers and you would say that they don't exist. But the farmers around Plum Village know very well that the sunflowers are already there. The seeds have been planted, the soil has been fertilized and watered, and all the other conditions necessary for the sunflowers to manifest are present, except one—the warmth of June and July. When that last condition is present, the sunflowers will manifest.

When causes and conditions are sufficient, we manifest. When they are lacking, we are latent. This is true of everyone—our father, mother, sister, brother, ourself, the person we love, the person we hate. When someone we love very much dies, the best thing we can do to ease our suffering is to look deeply and see that nothing is and nothing is not. The person we loved yesterday does not appear to be there anymore. But to say that she no longer exists is just an imaginary construction of our discriminative mind. If we know how to look deeply, we will be able to perceive her presence.

Before you manifest yourself, we cannot describe you as not existing. After you have manifested, we cannot describe you as existing either. There is only manifestation and non-manifestation. The notions of being and nonbeing cannot be applied to you or to any other reality. To be or not to be, that is not the question. The moment of dying is not really a moment of cessation but a moment of continuation. If a dying person has this kind of insight, she will have no fear.

37

Causes

When a seed gives rise to a formation,
it is the primary cause.
The subject of perception depends on the object of perception.
This is an object as cause.

THERE ARE FOUR KINDS of conditions that help things to manifest. All phenomena have a seed in store consciousness. This is the seed cause, the cause as condition. If you plant a kernel of corn in the soil, it will bring about a corn plant. The seed, or kernel, is the primary cause (hetu-pratyaya). If a sunflower seed falls into the soil, it is a primary cause of the sunflower plant that will grow there. The primary cause, however, is not enough on its own to bring about the plant. Soil, air, sunshine, minerals, and water are also needed in order for the corn or sunflower to fully manifest. These are called supporting causes and are discussed in the next verse.

We have talked about how subject and object are dependent on each other. The subject is dependent on the object. This is an object as cause, the second condition. The object-cause is absolutely necessary in order for cognition to take place. There cannot be consciousness without an object of consciousness, and this is true for the store consciousness, manas, and all the other consciousnesses. If there is no object of perception, there will be no perception.

There cannot be a perceiver if there is no object to be perceived. Consciousness is possible only when subject and object manifest together. If there is no object of perception, there will be no perception.

Conditions also need to be continuous in order for the sunflower seed to grow into a strong plant and offer a sunflower. If there is an interruption during that process of growing, the sunflower will not become a reality of manifestation. We call this the condition of immediate continuity (*samanantara-pratyaya*), also discussed in the next verse.

38

Conditions

Conditions that are favorable or non-obstructing
are supporting causes.
The fourth type of condition
is the immediacy of continuity.

SUPPORTING CAUSES are the third condition for manifestation. Once you have sown a seed into the soil, it will need the heat and light of sunshine, the minerals in the soil, and rain in order to sprout and grow.

There are many kinds of causes and conditions that help things to manifest. There are conditions that appear to be favorable, and there are conditions that do not appear to be favorable. These two kinds of developing conditions—favorable and unfavorable—are supporting causes. Favorable developing conditions are those like the sunshine, rain, minerals, and the farmer's care that help the kernel of corn grow into a corn plant. An unfavorable condition for development appears to be an obstruction, but it does not necessarily result in an unwholesome outcome. Suppose someone wants to rob a house but there is a hurricane that prevents him from doing so. Because of this unfavorable condition, the seeds of greed in him could not develop and manifest into the harmful action of theft.

An obstacle may play the role of supporting cause. Sometimes when a condition seems to be unfavorable, we may think of it as an obstacle, but these unfavorable conditions may give us more wisdom and strength later on in order to succeed. If a human being does not encounter difficulties, he or she would not grow into maturity. This is how conditions that are unfavorable can sometimes also be supportive of growth.

During the lifetime of the Buddha, his cousin Devadatta caused him a lot of difficulty. Yet the Buddha always considered Devadatta to be a supporting cause of his success as a teacher. Without difficulties you cannot achieve greatness. Even when the suffering and difficulties within you look like obstructions, they can become supporting causes. Garbage transforms into compost, and compost is essential for the growth of flowers. Both favorable and obstructing conditions can be used to further growth.

The fourth type of condition is the immediacy of continuity. If a phenomenon did not exist in a previous moment, it could not exist in the succeeding moment. The condition of the previous moment is the condition for this moment. There is no interruption in the flow. There is no cutting off. If you pull up a rice plant after it has begun to grow, it cannot continue to grow. Even though all the supporting causes are still present—the rain, the sunshine, and the earth—the condition of continuity has been interrupted and growth is stopped. If while you are using a computer, the electricity goes off and you haven't saved your work, you lose everything. We need each moment to follow the previous moment immediately without interruption for the result—manifestation—to take place. This is true with learning, practice, and everything that manifests. Store consciousness and the other seven consciousnesses also need this kind of continuity in order to continue manifesting.

Every formation, every manifestation of a phenomenon, needs at least these four conditions in order to occur—the primary cause, the object cause, the supporting causes, and the immediacy of continuity.

39

True Mind

Interdependent manifestation has two aspects—
deluded mind and true mind.
Deluded mind is imaginary construction.
True mind is fulfilled nature.

INTERDEPENDENT MANIFESTATION—the manifestation of all phenomena—should be viewed as resulting from both deluded mind and true mind. When our mind is deluded it is overloaded with ignorance, illusion, anger, and fear. True mind is consciousness that has been transformed and has the capacity of touching ultimate reality. A manifestation based on deluded mind will bring suffering and confusion. When we see people who suffer a lot and have a lot of hatred, pain, and sorrow in their daily lives, this is a manifestation based on deluded collective consciousness. A group of people living happily together, smiling, loving, and supporting one another, is a manifestation of a true collective consciousness. They know how to look at and touch things in the light of interbeing and interdependence. This way of perceiving things opens the door to the ultimate dimension.

Deluded mind—wrong perception and the suffering that results from it—gives rise to a cycle of twelve causes and results, which are collectively referred to as "birth and death." The Sanskrit term for this cycle is pratitya-samutpada, Interdependent Co-Arising, which was discussed in Chapter Fifteen. Here again are the twelve links of Interdependent Co-Arising. Each link or cause (*nidana*) gives rise to the next: ignorance (avidya); impulses (samskara); consciousness (vijñana); body and mind, or name and form, (namarupa); the six bases (shadayatana); contact (sparsha); feeling (vedana); craving (trishna); grasping or attachment (upadana); becoming (bhava); birth (jati); and old age and death (jara-maranam). Each link of the cycle brings about the next one—ignorance leads to impulses, which give rise to consciousness, and so forth.

The first link in the cycle of Interdependent Co-Arising, ignorance (avidya), is deluded mind. The world of birth and death is brought about by deluded mind. Wrong impulses arise from this mind. Impulses, in turn, produce seeds that make up consciousness. The cycle of birth, old age, and death based on ignorance brings us much suffering.

There is also a world conditioned by true mind. This world has sunlight, bird song, the wind in the pine trees—just as in the world we see around us—but it does not have being and nonbeing, coming and going, same and different, birth and death. The world that has true mind as its seed cause is the world of the Avatamsaka Sutra, where the one encompasses the all, where there can be no fear. True mind is the means for understanding birthlessness and deathlessness.

Much has been said about the cycle of Interdependent Co-Arising that is based on ignorance. But very little has been said about Interdependent Co-Arising based on true mind. The Buddha said that when ignorance ends there is understanding, just as when night ends there is daylight. If we put an end to ignorance, understanding will be there. In the cycle of causes and conditions that is based on understanding, the impulses that bring about suffering are not present. The nature of awakening is the energy that gives rise to impulses that bring about wisdom. Deluded consciousness brings about the body and mind that suffer. Wisdom brings about the body and mind of a Buddha.

The teachings of Interdependent Co-Arising, therefore, should include a cycle based on true mind as well as a cycle based on deluded mind. The cycle based on understanding is the world of the Avatamsaka—the sun, flowers, animals, forests, and all things that are wonderful—not the world based on ignorance, where all these things are seen as unsatisfactory and there is always the craving for something else.

Deluded mind is caused and conditioned. True mind is also caused and conditioned. The world that manifests based on deluded mind is full of suffering. The world that manifests based on true mind is a world of happiness and peace. It is not necessary to get out of the world that arises from deluded mind in order to reach the world that arises from true mind. The world of true mind reveals itself when the world of deluded mind is latent. We only have to change the direction we are looking in for the wonderful Avatamsaka world, the world based on true mind, to appear.

Many sutras and commentaries, such as the Treatise on the Awakening of Faith by Asvaghosa, speak of "two doors"—the door of birth and death and the door of suchness. These are equivalent to the historical and ultimate dimensions. Life has two faces: one is of birth, death, and suffering; the other is of suchness and happiness. The same sun shines each day, yet one day we are joyful and the next day we suffer. If our heart is burdened, our world is one of suffering. If our heart is light and open, unfettered by internal formations, the world is beautiful. True mind conditions the world of suchness and happiness, because it is not caught in attachment.

The Manifestation Only teachings describe reality as having three natures. The ultimate "fulfilled nature" (*nishpanna svabhava*) is the basis that lacks nothing. This is nirvana, the realm of suchness. The "constructed nature" (*parikalpita svabhava*) means constructed by thought. This is deluded mind, the world of imaginary construction. Deluded mind (*parikalpita*) is the mind that is conditioned by duality and notions of self and permanence, caught by ignorance, craving, and anger. Its nature is obscured. It is not light and clear. It conceives of being and nonbeing, coming and going, same and different, birth and death.

Deluded mind depends on a way of thinking based on pairs of opposites, notions, and ideas. It is not able to touch reality-in-itself. Because our deluded mind invents, creates, and constructs things that we cannot touch in reality, we live in a world of imaginary construction. All that we perceive is in the realm of representations, not the realm of suchness, the realm of things-in-themselves.

If your mind is clouded with ideas or notions, you cannot see things directly. During a retreat for Vietnam War veterans many years ago, one man told us that for many years he could only see a Vietnamese person as a threat, an enemy. When he first arrived at the retreat and saw me, a Vietnamese monk, he believed that I was his enemy. Later, thanks to the practice, he discovered that this was not true.

Another student once told me that he can accept that life and death are happening in each moment of our daily life—that life and death inter-are—

but he wondered whether it is possible for us to continue after our body disintegrates. He asked, "How can the brain imagine after it disintegrates, and, therefore, how can we conceive of a continuation?" If you look deeply in the present moment, you can see. Each of my students carries me within himself or herself. Right now in the city of Moscow, someone is breathing and smiling. That is me.

The air is filled with signals sent to us by satellites. If we have a television or a radio, we can help these signals manifest. But when we don't have a TV or radio, are the signals nonexistent? The Buddha said, "When conditions are sufficient, something manifests, and you consider it as existing. When conditions are not sufficient, something does not manifest, and you conceive of it as not existing." The key is manifestation. Everything manifests from our collective and individual store consciousness. But because we are caught in the notions of being and nonbeing, we cannot touch the ultimate dimension. We perceive things according to the patterns of our mind, the mental formations that manifest from seeds in our store consciousness, and therefore everything we see is distorted.

That is why meditating on our perceptions is so important. We create a world full of illusions and, as a result, we suffer in our day-to-day life. The solution is to learn to look with the eyes of wisdom, the true mind, the eyes of the Buddha. True mind arises from the fulfilled nature of reality. When we are able to perceive things clearly and directly, when we can touch the realm of things-in-themselves, our mind has become true mind.

True mind is radiant and wise. Understanding and compassion are there. When we see with the eyes of true mind, Interdependent Co-Arising brings about the wonderful world of the Avatamsaka, where everything is light, joyful, and pleasant. Interdependent Co-Arising can bring together a number of people who have understanding and love, and a small paradise can be built for the enjoyment of each member of that community. Imagine many Buddhas and bodhisattvas coming together to build a world filled with sunshine, joy, and peace. Visualize a community where people are understanding, loving, and not subject to wrong perceptions. This is the wonderful atmosphere of the Avatamsaka, the interdependent manifestation of wisdom (prajña), not of deluded mind (*parikalpita*).

When people with a deluded mind come together, they manifest suffering, anger, and hate. The collective manifestation they create is hell. That is why we practice looking deeply in order to transform delusion, anger, and hatred. The goal of the practice is not to end a life that is full of suffering, but to create a life filled with joy and peace.

40

The Realm of Suchness

Construction impregnates the mind with seeds of delusion,
bringing about the misery of samsara.
The fulfilled opens the door of wisdom
to the realm of suchness.

OUR CONSCIOUSNESS constructs and imagines all kinds of things. The constructed nature cuts up reality into separate parts: this is different from that; I am not you. Its function is to discriminate—self and other, inside and out, coming and going, birth and death. We tend to live our daily lives in the light of imaginary constructions that increase our delusion, and our habit energies are determined by these constructions. With this kind of discrimination, imagination, and construction, we water seeds of delusion in our consciousness every day and bring about the misery of samsara, the vicious cycle of suffering and delusion. Hell is constructed by us.

The fulfilled nature means to see things in the nature of interbeing, to live in such a way that we see the one in the many and the many in the one, and recognize that there is no birth, no death, no coming, no going. If we learn to look in this way, gradually the wonderful world of suchness will be revealed to us and the door of liberation will open. When we are able to touch the fulfilled nature of reality we can open the door of wisdom and establish ourselves in the realm of suchness, free from all delusion and suffering.

If we continue to look at things based on ideas of self, permanence, and duality, we will continue to water the seeds of delusion within us and continue to suffer in the cycle of samsara. That is why it is essential to change our way of looking. This new way of looking is paratantra svabhava—the nature of interdependence. Changing our way of looking, learning to see the interdependent nature of reality, is the basic practice. The next section of verses offers us ways to learn how to practice perceiving reality in this way.

Part VI

The Path of Practice

Verses Forty-One through Fifty describe the way to practice. Meditation on the nature of interdependence can transform delusion into illumination. With the daily training of looking deeply, of using our mindfulness to shed light on the interdependent nature of things, we can get rid of our tendency to perceive things as permanent and having a separate self. With this illumination, we see that the world of birth and death, the world of samsara, has the same ground as the realm of suchness, nirvana. Samsara and suchness are not separate from each other. They are two dimensions of one reality. If we are able to look deeply into even a single formation belonging to the world of samsara, we can break through and touch the ground of suchness.

The purpose of meditation is to touch the ground of no birth and no death, the realm of suchness. A Zen parable tells of an eleventh-century disciple who asked his master, "Where can I touch the reality of no birth and no death?" The master replied, "Right in the world of birth and death." By touching deeply the wave, you touch the water. By touching the world of samsara, you touch the world of suchness. We have been given the tools we need to touch the realm of suchness right here in samsara.

41

The Way to Practice

Meditating on the nature of interdependence
can transform delusion into enlightenment.
Samsara and suchness are not two.
They are one and the same.

WHEN WE LIVE in mindfulness, we are able to see the interdependent nature at the heart of things and transform our ignorance into insight. Delusion becomes enlightenment—we see that what we formerly perceived as samsara is really none other than nirvana, the realm of suchness. Mindfulness of the nature of interdependence is the key to this transformation.

Verses Thirty-Nine and Forty introduced us to the three natures. The Manifestation Only teachings say that all phenomena have one or more of three "self-natures" (svabhava)—the nature of imaginary construction and discrimination (parikalpita), the nature of interdependence (paratantra), and fulfilled nature (nishpanna), i.e., the nature of ultimate reality. Most of the time we are operating within the world of imaginary construction. We see things being born and dying, becoming and fading, one or many, coming and going, and in our mind we attribute these qualities to reality—but they are not reality itself. That is why they are called "imaginary constructions." Reality takes on the shape it does because of our lack of understanding. If we are sad, we see the moon as sad. The sad self-nature of the moon is a construction of our own mind. We are imprisoned by the world of ignorance, birth, and death because we take this imaginary, constructed world created by our mind as reality.

The opposite of the world of imaginary construction is the fulfilled self-nature, the nature of things as they are. This is not a construction of our mind nor is it subject to conceptualization. In the realm of things-in-themselves, there is no birth, no death, no one, no many, no coming, no going, no existence, no nonexistence. This is the ultimate dimension, the realm of suchness, nirvana. How do we leave the world of imaginary construction and enter nirvana? The way is through meditating on the nature of interdependence, the practice of paratantra.

Paratantra is the process of learning and training ourselves to look deeply into the nature of interdependence. When we see the interdependent self-nature of things, we are no longer caught in notions of duality. We see that samsara and suchness are one, not two. With deluded mind, we only see samsara. But when our mind is purified and becomes true mind, samsara is transformed into suchness, nirvana. Whether the ground beneath our feet is heaven or hell depends entirely on our way of seeing and walking. Samsara and suchness have the same ground—the ground of our consciousness, our mind. If we practice looking deeply into the nature of interdependence, the nature of interbeing of all things, that is paratantra. Through this insight we are able to transform delusion into illumination.

Interdependence means that a thing can arise only in reliance on other things. A flower arises in dependence on the seed, clouds, rain, soil, and the warmth of the sun. All these things are other than the flower, but the flower depends on them for its existence. This is the interdependent self-nature of a flower. Everything in the universe has this interdependent self-nature. Looking deeply and shining light on the interdependent self-nature of all that we perceive is the way to transform ignorance into awakened understanding.

We shine light on the way things are by looking deeply at impermanence, nonself, and interbeing. The Discourse on the Dharma Seal teaches that when we are able to touch the impermanent and nonself nature of phenomena, we can touch nirvana.[30] Another way of understanding or describing nirvana is the nature of interbeing of all things, or Interdependent Co-Arising. Impermanence and nonself belong to the phenomenal world; nirvana belongs to the noumenal world. The Three Dharma Seals of imper-

30 Taisho Tripitaka 104.

manence, nonself, and nirvana are the keys to understanding the Manifestation Only teachings.

The first key is impermanence, and it is used to open the door of reality concerning time. Nonself, the second key, is used to open the door of reality concerning space. They are spoken of as different but in truth they are one. Time and space are one. One cannot be without the other. The third key, nirvana, is the fulfilled nature, the reality of no birth, no death; no coming, no going; no one, no many; no existing, no not-existing. This is the world of Interdependent Co-Arising, where nothing exists as a separate, permanent entity. Impermanence and nonself go together with the nature of interbeing. To touch nirvana, to see the interdependent nature of reality, we have to touch impermanence and nonself.

The nature of imaginary construction goes together with our deluded beliefs in permanence and a separately existing self. We see the world around us as permanent and consisting of separate self-existing entities. That is why when we begin the practice we need to use the two keys of impermanence and nonself to shine light on the Interdependent Co-Arising nature of all things. The way to practice is to light the lamp of mindfulness and live every moment in its light.

Looking at a flower in the light of mindfulness, we can easily see that it arises in dependence with sunlight, rain, soil, and so on. We can do the same with human beings—looking at our parents or our friends, we also see their interdependent nature. We need to have the understanding of Interdependent Co-Arising when we look into our own and others' psychological traits. If someone is always angry or sad, we feel uncomfortable with that person, and we have the tendency to blame or shun him. But once we understand the roots of his anger and sadness, once we see how it manifests in dependence on other factors, we will be able to accept him, to look at him with compassion, and we will want to help him. Naturally, we and the other person will suffer less. This is the fruit that can be realized right away due to insight into Interdependent Co-Arising.

When we see a child who is well-behaved, we may understand the source and reason for his good behavior—is the ground that nutured him, his community and his family. It is even more important to see the interdependently co-arising nature of a child who is cruel. Just as with good behavior, the reasons for a child's cruelty can be found in his family, society, school, friends, and ancestors. If we do not shine the light of Interdependent Co-Arising on the child's character, we get angry or afraid, and we blame him. We must do our best to understand his interdependent self-nature in order to understand him, accept him, love him, and help him transform.

If we look at the death penalty in the light of Interdependent Co-Arising, we see that such an extreme punishment is not reasonable. A person commits a serious crime because of, among other things, the seeds he has inherited from his ancestors and the seeds that have been planted during his own lifetime. He has been exposed to various environments, and his parents, siblings, friends, educators, authorities, and society have not done enough to help him transform the unwholesome seeds that he has received. The ripening of those seeds has created a tremendous force in him that has driven him to kill, rape, or commit other serious crimes. When we think there is nothing to be done with that person other than to kill him, we manifest our collective powerlessness. As a society, we are defeated. We must look deeply at all the causes and conditions that helped make the criminal what he is so that we are able to give rise to a heart of compassion and help transform the unwholesome seeds in him as well as in our collective consciousness.

Of course, it is very difficult to forgive the person who harms us. Our first response is often anger and a desire for revenge. If, however, we are able to look deeply in the light of Interdependent Co-Arising, we may be able to see that if we had grown up, been educated, or experienced life the way that that criminal had, we would not be very different from him. When we understand this, we may even begin to feel protective toward him instead of angry or vengeful.

The Jataka Tales are stories of the previous lives of the Buddha. As a bodhisattva, he practiced inclusiveness and forbearance. There are stories of him smiling while his body is being sawed into pieces. As a young boy I read the Jataka Tales and I could not understand how a human being could be that patient and forgiving. I was too young to understand that the Buddha was able to practice that way because he had the eyes of understanding and could see the causes and conditions that had led to the cruelty and inhumanity of the person who was harming him. "The ability to see" is the raw material in a bodhisattva that leads to great compassion. Someone who has not looked deeply and has not yet tasted great compassion cannot understand the inclusiveness of a bodhisattva. But when, having looked deeply, we get even a small taste of compassion, we are able to understand and love those who are cruel and irresponsible. We are able to understand the smile of the bodhisattva.

During the war in Vietnam, many monks, nuns, and young laypeople gave assistance to the victims of war. Our young social workers were greatly motivated by love. They saw their people and their land suffering, and they wanted to help. The environment in which they worked was wretched and filled with suffering. One side thought we were communists and wanted to kill us. The other side thought we were enemy sympathizers or CIA agents. Many workers died during that time of darkness. In 1966, after I had already left Vietnam, I suffered a great deal when I received news of the killings. I did not know whether our social workers were capable of reconciling in their own minds with the killers. So I wrote this poem of advice.

Promise me,
promise me this day,
promise me now,
while the sun is overhead
exactly at the zenith,
promise me:
Even as they
strike you down
with a mountain of hatred and violence;
even as they step on you and crush you
like a worm,
even as they dismember and disembowel you,
remember, brother,
remember:
man is not our enemy.
The only thing worthy of you is compassion—

invincible, limitless, unconditional.
Hatred will never let you face
the beast in man.
One day, when you face this beast alone,
with your courage intact, your eyes kind,
untroubled
(even as no one sees them),
out of your smile
will bloom a flower.
And those who love you
will behold you
across ten thousand worlds of birth and dying.
Alone again,
I will go on with bent head,
knowing that love has become eternal.
On the long, rough road,
the sun and the moon
will continue to shine.[31]

Before I wrote this poem I spent a long time looking deeply. If we are not reconciled with our killers at the time of death, it is extremely painful to die. When we feel reconciled and have some compassion for them, we suffer much less. One of my students, Nhat Chi Mai, immolated herself as a call to the two warring parties to sit down together and end the war. Before she set fire to herself she read this poem into a tape recorder twice. When we look deeply into the nature of interdependence and see that the person harming us is also a victim—of his family, his society, his environment—understanding arises naturally. With understanding there is empathy and reconciliation. Understanding always leads to love. When we have love and compassion, we do not have anger and we do not suffer. Our fear, anxiety, sorrow, despair, and hopelessness are what cause us to suffer. The ability to see the interdependent nature of all things leads to compassion in our hearts and keeps us from suffering, even when people betray us and cause

31 Thich Nhat Hanh, "Recommendation," in *Call Me by My True Names*, p. 18.

us harm. When we are able to love others in spite of their misdeeds, we are already a bodhisattva.

Compassion grows in us from even the smallest acts. If while practicing walking meditation we see that we are about to step on a worm and we stop to avoid it, we know that compassion is already in us. If we practice looking deeply and live our daily lives in an awakened way, our compassion will grow day by day. A phrase in the Lotus Sutra encapsulates this: "Looking at all beings with the eyes of compassion." When we look at trees, rocks, clouds, sky, humans, and animals with the eyes of love, we know that understanding is already there. Understanding is the fruit of looking deeply, of shining the light of awareness on things. Understanding, love, and compassion are one.

Through the practice of deep looking, we can see the interdependent nature of all things and transform delusion into illumination. The object of deluded mind is samsara. The object of true mind is nirvana. When we are able to transform deluded mind into true mind through the practice of paratantra, of seeing the nature of interbeing of all things, we reach the realm of suchness, the realm of things-in-themselves. If we know how to walk with solidity and freedom, the ground under our feet is heaven. If we walk with sorrow, fear, and anger, we walk in hell. It all depens on our way of walking, our way of being.

When you look deeply into birth and death, you see the nature of no-birth and no-death. It is like the water and the wave. We think that there is one moment when the wave begins and one moment when it ceases to be, and so we get caught in the fear of birth and death. Birth and death, wave and water, are just appearances, just notions. We have other notions, like higher and lower, or more or less beautiful. Because of these notions, we suffer. This is samsara.

When we touch the reality of interdependence, the reality of the fulfilled nature (*nishpanna*), we are free from all notions, including notions of coming and going, being and nonbeing, birth and death. We realize non-fear when we are able to touch nirvana. It is the greatest relief to touch the ultimate dimension, nirvana, and this is possible through the practice of looking deeply. Don't think that it is too difficult. We all have the chance to touch nirvana, to see things globally and not be caught in the small view.

Suppose yesterday someone said something that hurt you deeply. He did not give you a chance to reply. He just left. You were so angry. You felt that you had lost your dignity, because you did not have a chance to reply. All afternoon you suffered. But this morning, while you are brushing your teeth, you burst out laughing. The whole matter that had caused you so much suffering suddenly seems insignificant. Only one night separates you from the event, and yet already you feel that kind of relief, because you are going in the direction of seeing the bigger picture. If we know how to look globally, how to touch time and space as a whole, we will not suffer.

When your beloved says something that hurts you, try this practice: Close your eyes, breathe mindfully in and out, and visualize the two of you one hundred years from now. After three breaths, when you open your eyes, you will no longer feel hurt; instead, you will want to hug her. These are examples of touching nirvana. We learn to touch the whole and not get caught in small situations. Imaginary construction brings about the misery of samsara. The nature of nirvana opens the door of wisdom and reveals the realm of suchness. The bridge between the two is paratantra, insight into the interdependent co-arising nature of reality.

Samsara and suchness are not different. They have the same ground. The wave does not have to do anything to become water. It is already water. It has had nirvana in it for a long time. Just like the water, you don't have to look for nirvana. When you are able to see through the eyes of interbeing and interdependence, you touch the nature of nirvana within yourself.

42

Flower and Garbage

Even while blooming, the flower is already in the compost,
and the compost is already in the flower.
Flower and compost are not two.
Delusion and enlightenment inter-are.

THE FORTY-SECOND VERSE helps us bring the teaching of interbeing into our everyday lives. "Flower" and "garbage" are images used to describe the interdependent nature of ignorance and awakening. We usually think that awakening has nothing to do with ignorance. We put it on one side of the fence and ignorance on the other, fearing that ignorance might otherwise contaminate awakening. But in truth they cannot be separated in this way. If there were no ignorance and confusion, there could be no awakening. Ignorance is the ground from which awakening is cultivated. If you say, "I want to put an end to the cycle of birth and death. I will only accept liberation," it shows that you do not yet understand the nature of Interdependent Co-Arising.

If you try to throw away "this" to be able to find "that," you will never find what you are searching for. "That" can only be found within "this." The Buddha advises us not to run away from anything in order to run toward something else. In fact, the practice of Buddhism is the practice of aimlessness, of having no goal (*apranihita*). If we are pure, calm, and clear in our mind, then we are already in the Pure Land. Ignorance and awakening are interdependent. Nirvana can only be found within the world of birth and death. Roots of affliction (klesha), the unwholesome mental formations, such as greed, hatred, ignorance, pride, doubt, and views, cause us to suffer. When we want awakening, we take hold of our mental formations in order to transform them.

If we are about to die of thirst and someone brings us a glass of muddy water, we know we have to find a way of filtering it in order to survive. We can't just throw it away; that water, even though it is not pure, is our only hope of salvation. In the same way, we have to accept all our afflictions, our mental formations, all the difficulties in the world, our body, and our mind, in order to transform them. If we reject them, if we try to run away from them, we will never succeed. There is no escaping the things we hate. We can only transform them into what we love.

A gardener who is aware of the reality of interbeing will not throw away her garbage. Looking at a heap of garbage, she can already see cucumbers, lettuce, and flowers in it. She will use it to make compost for her garden. The interdependent nature of the flower means that a flower is made of non-flower elements, such as garbage. If we remove the element "garbage" from the flower, the flower cannot exist. The flower is on its way to becoming garbage, and the garbage is also on its way to becoming a flower. When we take hold of our afflictions and use them as compost, the flowers of joy, peace, liberation, and happiness will grow. We must accept what is here and now, including our suffering and our delusion. Accepting our suffering and delusion already brings us some peace and joy. This is the beginning of practice.

We accept what is in the present moment in order to have a deep perspective and the capacity to transform our circumstances. If we always make the aim of our practice some future circumstance or result, we will never learn to accept the present time and place, which in fact are the correct conditions for our practice. Flowers and garbage both exist in the present, here and now. The conditions for enlightenment also exist here and now, in the present. Enlightenment cannot be found by running away from delusion. Looking deeply into the nature of delusion, you touch enlightenment.

In our store consciousness is a wonderful seed called mindfulness, the capacity to be aware of what is happening in the present moment. That seed may be weak, because we seldom water it. Generally, we do not go about our lives in a mindful way. We do not eat mindfully. We do not walk mindfully. We do not look at or speak to people mindfully. We live in forgetfulness. But always there is the opportunity to live our life fully. When we drink water, we can be aware that we are drinking water. When we walk, we can be aware that we are walking. Mindfulness is available to us in every moment.

Although our seed of mindfulness may be weak, it can grow quickly if we practice doing things mindfully. In order to grow, mindfulness needs nourishment. We all have seeds of mindfulness, loving kindness, understanding, and joy in us. These seeds can become beautiful flowers if we can learn how to transform the garbage of our hatred, discrimination, despair, and anger. By looking deeply into the nature of suffering and transforming the energy of suffering in us, we can help the energy of happiness and peace to manifest.

43

Interbeing

Don't run away from birth and death.
Just look deeply into your mental formations.
When the true nature of interdependence is seen,
the truth of interbeing is realized.

NO BIRTH AND NO DEATH lie right in the heart of birth and death. As long as we run away from birth and death. we will never reach the realm of birthlessness and deathlessness. When we stop and look deeply into our mental formations, our notions of self and other, birth and death, ignorance and awakening, then we see their true self-nature of interdependence. That is interbeing.

In order to look deeply, however, we need the energy of mindfulness. Mindfulness is like a generator that produces electricity. From the electricity created by the generator comes light, the energy of heat for cooking, and many other benefits. We need to practice in a way that produces the power of mindfulness in our daily life. When we live mindfully, observing deeply what is in us and around us, we realize the nature of Interdependent Co-Arising, the interpenetration of all things.

If we are skillful, we can touch nirvana with our insight into Interdependent Co-Arising, impermanence, and nonself. We see that nirvana lies right here in the present moment—in the table, the chair, the house, the mountain, the cloud, and each cell of our body. Some Christian theologians say that the Kingdom of God lies right in our hearts, that we can touch it at any time. Nirvana is the same. When we are caught in ideas like permanence and self, we cannot touch nirvana. The moment we touch nirvana, we are free from birth and death.

The Buddha taught that there are Five Powers. First is the power of faith.

We need to have faith in the possibility of touching nirvana, of awakening to suchness. This is not blind faith, it is based on our understanding, insight, and experience. Faith leads to energy, the second power. Without faith and confidence, we easily get tired. To have the energy to look deeply into things, we need to have confidence in our capacity for awakening, and faith in the awakened understanding of the Buddha. We transform our energy into mindfulness, the third power. Where there is mindfulness, there is concentration, the fourth power.

When we live in mindfulness, everything takes place in the concentration of looking deeply. We can see the interdependent co-arising nature of things within and around us. When our concentration is weak, we might be able to see their interdependent nature for a short time, but we soon fall back into seeing things as permanent and having a separate self. But with strong and steady concentration, we can continue to see the nature of interbeing of things within and around us. When our concentration is great, it leads to the fifth power, understanding. With understanding we don't spend time dreaming of the future or dwelling in the past. We wake up to our true mind. With one mindful step, we enter the Realm of Suchness or the Kingdom of God. Understanding, in turn, strengthens our faith. The Five Powers help each other.

Generating the energy of mindfulness is essential for the practice. We have to live each moment of our life mindfully. We look, listen, and touch with our mindfulness. When we cook, we cook mindfully, aware of our breathing and what we are doing. Enjoying our breathing in whatever we are doing, we produce the energy of mindfulness to help us touch life deeply. Meditation helps us obtain insight, dissipating our misunderstanding and ignorance, and brings about love, acceptance, and joy. There is no need for us to run away from birth and death. There is no need to run away from our garbage. We can learn the art of taking care of our suffering and transforming it into peace, joy, and loving kindness. If suffering, fear, or despair is there, adopt the attitude of non-fear. Learn the techniques of transforming the garbage of the afflictions into flowers of well-being, solidity, and freedom.

Looking deeply into a flower, we see the interbeing of the flower. Looking deeply into the garbage, we see the interbeing of the garbage. Looking deeply is not speculating. We have to practice. We have to be concentrated. We have to be present in order to touch the flower deeply, to really experience its nature of interbeing. When we live mindfully, everything reveals the nature of interbeing. Looking deeply at a leaf, we touch the sunshine, the river, the ocean, and our mind in it. This is true practice.

The teachings of impermanence and nonself are not doctrines or subjects for a philosophical discussion. They are instruments for meditation, keys to help us unlock the door of reality. When someone offers us a hammer for our carpentry work, we should not put it on an altar and worship it. We must learn how to use it. Don't be dogmatic about impermanence and nonself. Practice looking deeply and touch the nature of interdependence, the nature of interbeing, in reality.

44

Right View

Practice conscious breathing
to water the seeds of awakening.
Right View is a flower
blooming in the field of mind consciousness.

THIS VERSE offers a complete method of practice to water the seeds of enlightenment that we all have within us. In our store consciousness we have seeds of ignorance and delusion, but we also have seeds of understanding and compassion.

The object of our faith is the seed of awakening that lies within our store consciousness. This is not blind faith. It can be experienced directly. Awakening means mindfulness. Mindfulness is the water that nourishes the *bodhi* seed, the seed of awakening. If in our daily lives we practice mindfulness in order to look deeply at things, one day Right View will bloom like a flower permanently and not just from time to time in our mind consciousness.

Right View is the first practice of the Noble Eightfold Path, which also includes Right Thinking, Right Speech, Right Action, Right Livelihood, Right Effort, Right Mindfulness, and Right Concentration.[32] Right View is the clear vision of the mind consciousness which is the gardener doing the watering. While eating, walking, washing, or cooking, the clear view of our mind consciousness waters the seed of bodhi, awakening, with the water of Right Mindfulness. Mindfulness is the water that nourishes the bodhi seed. The more mindfulness it receives, the more it grows. The more it grows, the more confidence we have in the practice. With the continuous practice of

32 For an in-depth discussion of the Eightfold Path, see Thich Nhat Hanh, *The Heart of the Buddha's Teaching*, chaps. 9–16.

mindfulness, the sprout will grow into a beautiful bodhi tree. Wherever there is a bodhi tree, there is a Buddha. The seed of awakening gives rise to the seed of love. Only mindfulness can lead to a breakthrough in understanding, where before there was confusion and darkness.

Remember, mind consciousness is the gardener who waters the seeds in the store consciousness. The gardener has to have confidence in the earth and be diligent in watering. Our only task is to plant the bodhi seed in the earth of store consciousness and water it with mindfulness. Naturally, the seed of awakening will flower in our mind consciousness. No other effort is needed. Our only task is to practice mindfulness. Store consciousness does the rest. One day, on waking up or on hearing someone say something, there will be a breakthrough, an awakening. You will suddenly understand things that until then have remained obscure. When a Zen master assigns you a koan, plant it in your store consciousness. Don't leave it in your mind consciousness for your intellect to think about. Entrust your koan to the earth of store consciousness and the earth will look after it for you.

We might chant a sutra for twenty years without understanding a word of it, and then one day, reading a certain line, we *see*. That is awakened understanding, the flower that blooms in our mind consciousness. Awakening is possible if while chanting the sutra we are aware of what we are chanting. How many times do we chant a sutra without understanding a word of it? If you chant a sutra and know that you are chanting a sutra, mindfulness is there. When you drink a glass of water and know that you are drinking a glass of water, mindfulness is there. If you continue to cultivate that kind of awareness in your daily life, it will grow into a tall, beautiful bodhi tree that shelters you, and one day understanding and insight will be born.

Understanding is not something we receive from someone else, even a teacher. The most our teacher can do is help us touch the seed of understanding that lies deep within our store consciousness. Once that seed is watered, understanding will bloom like a flower in our mind consciousness. Understanding is Right View, the fruit of the practice. We begin with a tiny Right View, but as we continue to practice, our Right View increases, and the other seven aspects of the Eightfold Path increase also. As our Right

View grows, our practice improves. And as our practice improves, our Right View grows.

Most of us begin the practice with a view of impermanence and nonself that is quite theoretical. But with mindful looking and mindful living, we will discover the essence of impermanence and nonself, the true nature of interbeing, and our Right View will become true and deep. The seed of Right View is the seed of insight. If we know how to practice mindful breathing and mindful looking and we water the seed of enlightenment in our store consciousness, one morning it will spring up and bloom like a flower in the field of our mind consciousness.

Conscious breathing is the basis of the practice of mindfulness. We identify the in-breath as in-breath and the out-breath as out-breath: "Breathing in, I know I am breathing in. Breathing out, I know I am breathing out." For twenty-six hundred years, generations of Buddhist practitioners have used this method. Before we begin the practice of conscious breathing, our body is here but our mind is somewhere else. The moment we breathe mindfully we bring body and mind together. Suddenly touching life in the present moment becomes possible.

Life is filled with suffering but it also contains many wonders. If you want to touch the wonders of life, come back to the present moment. Practice conscious breathing and you will find yourself in the here and the now. If you were not here, how could life be real and true? If you are distracted, real life is not possible. Your true presence makes life possible, and it cannot be bought. It can only be obtained with practice—the practice of mindful walking, mindful breathing, and mindful sitting.[33] The practice of mindfulness is the practice of being present.

Our capacity to be present has tremendous consequences in our daily lives, in our relationships with others. The greatest gift that we can offer to our beloved is our true presence. Practice walking meditation, sitting meditation, and breathing mindfully to be present for your beloved. When she suffers, practice conscious breathing and say to her, "Darling, I know that

33 For more on walking meditation, see Thich Nhat Hanh, *The Long Road Turns to Joy: A Guide to Walking Meditation* (Berkeley, CA: Parallax Press, 1996). For more on sitting meditation, see Thich Nhat Hanh, *Breathe! You Are Alive: Sutra on the Full Awareness of Breathing*, Revised Edition (Berkeley, CA: Parallax Press, 1996).

you suffer. That is why I am here for you." If you suffer, you have to practice breathing in and out and say, "Darling, I suffer. Please help." When you love someone, there must also be trust. If you suffer, you should be able to go to those you love and tell them that you suffer and need their help. In true love, there is no room for pride or arrogance. Go to him and tell him that you suffer and need his help. If you cannot, something is wrong in your relationship. It is important to practice this. Without true presence, how can you love and care for one another? You generate the energy of mindfulness in order to be truly present.

The most beautiful declaration of love is, "Darling, I am here for you." When you pronounce this mantra, there will be a transformation in both of you. This is the practice of mindfulness.

45

Mindfulness

When sunlight shines,
it helps all vegetation grow.
When mindfulness shines,
it transforms all mental formations.

THANKS TO THE SUN, vegetables can grow. There are other conditions for the growth of plants, like rain and soil, but the sun is the primary source of energy that allows living things to grow. Whatever food we eat—whether or not we are vegetarian—we are eating the energy of the sun. Sunlight nourishes us all.

Just as the sunlight provides the energy for the wonderful transformation of a seed into a plant that nourishes us, mindfulness is the energy that is able to transform all other mental formations (chitta-samskara). Mindfulness itself is one of the wholesome mental formations, belonging to the group of the five particular mental formations that also include zeal, determination, concentration, and insight. In the light of interbeing, each mental formation contains every other mental formation. When mindfulness arises, it is able to transform other mental formations, just as the sun is able to transform vegetables and, in fact, transform the face of the Earth. Mindfulness is like the sun. It only has to shine its light to do its work. Just as vegetables are photosensitive and able to receive sunlight, mental formations are able to receive the light of mindfulness.

The practice is not to get rid of our afflictions, our unwholesome mental formations. The more we try to repress them, the more they will grow. We have to accept them and touch them with the light of mindfulness. This touching will bring about their transformation. The secret of practice is the ability to shine the light of mindfulness on the field of our mind consciousness, so that when mental formations, such as anger, appear in this field, they are met with the energy of mindfulness. When anger arises, we do not suppress it. Instead, we invite mindfulness to touch it. We say, "Breathing in, I know I am angry." Two things are present: anger and mindfulness. If we can nourish our mindfulness for a period of time, our anger will be recognized, embraced, and transformed to a greater or lesser extent depending on the strength of our mindfulness. Without mindfulness, we lose our way, drifting along on waves of suffering. When there is mindfulness, we know which direction we want to go in order to transform ourselves.

The Buddha taught his followers to recite the Five Remembrances every day:

1) I am of the nature to grow old. There is no way to escape growing old.

2) I am of the nature to have ill health. There is no way to escape having ill health.

3) I am of the nature to die. There is no way to escape death.

4) All that is dear to me and everyone I love are of the nature to change. There is no way to escape being separated from them.

5) My actions are my only true belongings. I cannot escape the consequences of my actions. My actions are the ground on which I stand.

It is important to understand this teaching of the Buddha in the light of the Manifestation Only teachings. If we look at the Five Remembrances only as ominous warnings of what is to come, they will serve only to create more suffering. Our practice is to smile to them, to look deeply and shine the light of mindfulness in order to transform our fear of old age, sickness, death, being separated from people and things we love, and to see the nature of our actions. The first four of the Five Remembrances address the fears that are always lying in the depths of our consciousness. However much we try to keep them down and forget them, they are still there. Instead of suppressing them, we invite them into our mind consciousness and smile to them, because we know these fears influence the activities of our mind consciousness.

When we practice this contemplation every day, we are inviting these seeds of fear to come up. When they come up we face them with mindfulness. If we are not mindful when seeds of fear come up, we will not be in control of the situation and we will suffer. That is why we contemplate our seeds of fear with Right Mindfulness. When we shine the light of mindfulness upon them, our fears lessen and one day they will be completely transformed.

The practice of the Five Remembrances helps us face our fears directly and not see them as enemies. They are us. Our happiness, our suffering, our love, and our anger are all us. We treat all mental formations in the same way, in the spirit of nonduality. We do not turn ourselves into a battleground, with one side fighting the other. Some traditions teach just that—the right must do battle to overcome the wrong. In Buddhism, we see both sides as ourselves and we try to accept and look after all parts of ourselves, recognizing their interdependent nature. Our afflictions, our unwholesome mental formations, must be accepted before they can be transformed. The more we fight them, the stronger they become. The more we repress them, the more significant they become.

What can we do to transform our deep-rooted seeds of suffering? There are three ways. The first way is that we allow them to lie quietly in our store consciousness while we sow new seeds and nourish existing seeds of peace, joy, and happiness. Our mind consciousness sends these seeds of peace and joy down to interact with the seeds of suffering and transform them. This is indirect transformation.

The second way is our continuous practice of mindfulness that allows us to recognize seeds of suffering when they arise. Every time seeds of suffering manifest as mental formations in our mind consciousness, we bathe them in the light of mindfulness. When they are in contact with mindfulness, they will weaken. Without mindfulness, we aren't even able to recognize these seeds of suffering. With mindfulness, we can recognize them and not be afraid.

If a bird has been hit by an arrow, whenever it sees a bow it will be afraid. It won't even perch on a branch that resembles the shape of a bow. If we were wounded as a young child, the seeds of suffering we received then are still with us today. The way we relate to life in the present moment is based on these seeds of suffering. Every day seeds from our past manifest in our mind consciousness, but because we have not bathed them in the light of mindfulness, we are not aware of them. With mindfulness, whenever those seeds sprout we are able to recognize them. "Oh, it's you! I know you." This recognition alone will cause them to lose some of their power over us. Our seeds of suffering are a field of energy, and mindfulness is also a field of energy. When these two fields meet, the seeds of suffering are transformed. Putting them in touch with mindfulness transforms them.

The third way to deal with the afflictions that have been with us since childhood is to deliberately invite them up into our mind consciousness. When our mindfulness is strong and stable, we do not have to wait for the seeds of suffering to arise unexpectedly. We know they are lying there in the basement of our store consciousness and we invite them up into our mind consciousness—when it is not occupied with other things and can shine the light of mindfulness on them. We invite the sadness, despair, regrets, and longings that in the past have been difficult for us to touch, and we sit down and talk with them, like old friends. But before we invite them up, we must be sure that the lamp of our mindfulness is lit and that its light is steady and strong.

If we practice all three ways to deal with our seeds of suffering, we will be stable. But someone who is suffering greatly and does not know how to practice mindfulness should not start out practicing the third way—inviting the seeds of suffering up into the conscious mind. He should first practice nourishing and giving rise to seeds of happiness. When he has made progress in the first method and more of the energy of mindfulness has been generated, he can try the second method, accepting and recognizing suffering when it arises. The more he is able to recognize the seeds of suffering, the weaker they become. Finally, when he feels strong enough, he can use the third method and invite the seeds of suffering up into his mind consciousness where mindfulness can touch and transform them.

Dealing with suffering is like handling a poisonous snake. We have to learn about the snake, and we ourselves have to grow stronger and more stable in order to handle it without harming ourselves. At the end of this process, we will be ready to confront the snake. If we never confront it, one day it will surprise us and we will die of a snakebite. The pain we carry in the deep levels of our consciousness is similar. When it grows big and confronts us, there is nothing we can do if we haven't practiced and become strong and stable in mindfulness. We should only invite our suffering up when we are ready. Then, when it comes, we can safely handle it. To transform our suffering, we do not struggle with it or try to get rid of it. We simply bathe it in the light of our mindfulness.

Through these teachings on Manifestation Only, we can see the truth of nonduality, interbeing, and nonviolence, both in learning about the practice and in our daily activities. With the energy of mindfulness, we can handle both the flowers and the garbage in us. With mindfulness, we protect the flowers and transform the garbage back into flowers. We are no longer afraid of our garbage. A bodhisattva knows how to transform his garbage back into flowers. A foolish person tries to run away from it. If we try to abandon our garbage, what kind of food will we have to nourish our flower?

There are moments when we are capable of seeing the nature of interbeing in people and things. But at other moments we forget and fall back into our world of imaginary construction. That is why continuous practice is important in order for the flower of enlightenment to bloom permanently in the field of our mind consciousness. Just as sunlight shines on vegetation and makes it grow, once mindfulness is lit up, it can transform all the other mental formations. Every mental formation is sensitive to the energy of mindfulness. When it is a wholesome mental formation, mindfulness will help it grow and flourish. When a mental formation is negative, the energy of mindfulness can transform it into something positive. Mindfulness is the very heart of our practice.

46

Transformation at the Base

We recognize internal knots and latent tendencies
so we can transform them.
When our habit energies dissipate,
transformation at the base is there.

WHEN WE ARE ROOTED in mindfulness, we can see clearly what is unfolding within us. We don't grasp at it and we don't push it away—we simply recognize it. When we are angry, mindfulness recognizes the anger. When we are jealous, mindfulness recognizes the jealousy. When we acknowledge the presence of fear or sadness in us, we don't judge it and say that it is bad. We simply observe every occurrence in our body and mind with our mindfulness, and greet whatever arises without praise, reprimand, or judgment. This is called "mere recognition." Mere recognition does not take sides. The object of recognition is not our enemy. It is none other than ourselves. We acknowledge it as we would acknowledge our own child.

In the Discourse on the Four Establishments of Mindfulness, the Buddha teaches us that there are four fields of practice—contemplating the body in the body, the feelings in the feelings, the mind in the mind, and the phenomena that arise as objects of mind in the objects of mind.[34] Mind here means all fifty-one mental formations. The eight consciousnesses can be compared to eight rivers, and the fifty-one mental formations to drops of water in those rivers. Although mind and objects of mind are considered two different fields, in fact, they are one. Mind is the perceiver and objects

34 See Thich Nhat Hanh, *Transformation & Healing: Sutra on the Four Foundations of Mindfulness* (Berkeley, CA: Parallax Press, 1990).

of mind are the perceived. But perceiver and perceived can never be separated; they make one whole. Objects of mind do not arise independently of mind. Objects of mind—including the body, the feelings, and all other mental formations—are products of mind.

The four fields of mindfulness—body, feelings, mind, and objects of mind—inter-are. Each field contains the other three. According to the practice taught in this sutra, we recognize every phenomenon in each of these four fields as it arises. Our principal task is recognizing. This is like the work of a doorman who greets everyone who comes in or goes out. We are the doorman for our six sense perceptions. If there is no doorman, the house is not guarded and can be invaded. We light the lamp of mindfulness so that we can see and recognize everything that is happening. In this way, the house is secure.

The eyes are a deep ocean,
With whirlpools and violent winds,
And shadows beneath the surface
And sea monsters deep within.
My boat is sailing in mindfulness,
I vow to hold the tiller firmly
So that I do not drown in an ocean of form.
Using my conscious breath,
I am guarding my eyes for my protection and yours.
So that today continues to be a beautiful day,
And tomorrow, we still have each other.[35]

Our sense bases—our eyes, ears, nose, tongue, body, and mind—are all deep oceans filled with danger. We can drown in the myriad sights, sounds, smells, tastes, tactile sensations, and thoughts that our senses take in. A practitioner who does not light the lamp of mindfulness to guard his or her six senses is not really able to practice.

With regard to the first field of mindfulness, our body, we are aware of

35 Thich Nhat Hanh, "Guarding the Six Senses," in *A Basket of Plums; Songs for the Practice of Mindfulness*, 2005 Edition (compiled by Joseph Emet, distributed by Parallax Press), No. 23.

our breathing, our standing, our walking, our sitting, and our lying down. If we are not aware of these things while we are doing them, we are not practicing. The second field of practice is our feelings. As soon as we have a feeling of sadness, joy, anger, fear, hatred, or despair, we recognize the feeling. If we do not, these feelings will influence us and our actions without our being aware that they are doing so. Because of an unrecognized feeling of anger, we may speak harshly to the person we love without even knowing it.

A philosopher asked the Buddha what his monks did all day long. The Buddha replied that they walked, stood, lay down, sat, ate, washed their bowls, and swept the floor. How, then, asked the philosopher, were they any different from people of the world? The Buddha replied that the difference was that his monks did these things in mindfulness, guarding their six senses. Whatever we are doing, we can be mindful. We can recognize all the phenomena in our body, our feelings, our mind, and the objects of our mind. We shouldn't think that because we are so busy we cannot practice. When we work in mindfulness, that is already right practice. Problems arise only when we do things without mindfulness.

Suppose we are looking at a tree—we have a pleasant feeling, enjoying the greenness and freshness of the tree. If we are able to strengthen the energy of mindfulness in us as we look at the tree, our pleasant feeling will increase, and the tree will become even brighter and clearer. In New England, the fall foliage of the forests is so beautiful that people visit this region just to see it, like a pilgrimage. But the beauty of the foliage that is perceived and the extent of each person's joy depends on their freedom and peace of mind. If someone's heart is at peace and his mindfulness is strong, his enjoyment of the foliage will be a thousand times greater than someone who is suffering and can see only the sorrow of his life. Each person can be looking at the same scenery, but they do not enjoy the same peace and happiness. The difference is their capacity for mindfulness.

A beautiful maple tree belongs to the field of objects of mind. The joy we feel belongs to the field of mind. If we do not recognize the tree's beauty, it is as if the tree and its beauty do not exist. Our suffering or our happiness lies in the field of feelings. Mindfulness is the doorman that guards our senses. Once we know how to use mindfulness to recognize the formations in our mind consciousness as they arise, we know the direction in which we must go. It is not even that we intentionally seek a direction—the fact that we are mindful shows us the direction, automatically. We will know whether what is happening is healthful or harmful, beneficial or not, and we will pursue it or try to avoid it.

There are internal knots and latent tendencies in all of us. Internal knots (*samyojana*) are the blocks of sadness and pain that are tied up in our consciousness. Their nature is unwholesome. When someone says something or we see something that makes us angry or sad, this can begin to create an internal knot. The Chinese character for samyojana means "to be ordered around." An internal knot lies in our store consciousness and makes us do things without our even knowing it. If we don't guard our six senses, there is no way to avoid the formation of internal knots. If we do not guard the sense base of the eyes when it comes into contact with form, sooner or later we will have an internal knot. We will become angry, sad, or attached.

Addiction is an internal knot. We do not start out being addicted to drugs, alcohol, or an unwholesome relationship. The knot is tied gradually. If internal knots announced themselves with a loud noise when they formed, we would know immediately that they were there. But we can't discern the moment when we became addicted to drugs or alcohol. We don't know exactly when we became infatuated with someone who is not good for us. The process of the formation of an internal knot happens stealthily. If we are guarding the six senses, however, as soon as we have a feeling of attachment, we will be aware of it. We know that we have a sweet feeling of attachment when we hold a glass of wine or a cigarette, or toward a person we should not be so close to. We know where this pleasant feeling is going to take us. With mindfulness—the recognition of what is happening as it is happening—the internal knot of attachment will not be able to form without our noticing it until it is too late.

Internal knots can lie quietly in our consciousness for a long time, but eventually they will arise and order us to do something. We do not want to act out our anger, we do not enjoy the sensation of our face turning red and our fist banging on the table, but the internal knot of anger is stronger than we are. When we are ordered around by an internal knot it is a crushing defeat for us. The way to avoid this is by recognizing our internal knots as they arise. Suppose I have just met someone, and quite spontaneously there arises in me a feeling of aversion for that person. If I am not mindful of this feeling of aversion, I will not be able to recognize it as an internal knot and I will continue to be pulled along by feelings of hatred. But if I live in mindfulness, as soon as the unpleasant feeling starts to manifest, I recognize it immediately: "I have an unpleasant feeling when I look at that person."

When we have the habit of recognizing what is going on in us, we follow this by looking deeply into what we have recognized. We will not forget about that feeling even after it has died down. We will continue to observe ourselves and to look deeply. We may discover that the person resembles someone who wronged us in the past, and because of this we have a complex about that person even though he himself has not done or said anything to hurt us. Our internal knot compels us to feel this way. Once we have observed it deeply, there will be some understanding of what is going on. This understanding is what leads to our liberation. We are free of the influence of our internal knot. Then we can talk to the person without any problem.

Latent tendencies (*anushaya*) are internal knots that have been partly transformed so that we think they are no longer there. It is as if we have cut down a tree but have left the roots: the tree may appear to be gone, but it still exists in latent form in the roots that remain underground. We cannot separate ourselves from latent tendencies. They are like the shadow that follows the form. When we practice the observation of nonself and interpenetration, we may think that we have pulled up the roots of being caught in the idea of self. But those roots were there before we were born and much more work still has to be done to transform them. We must be careful and recognize the latent tendency of attachment to self when it arises in one form or another.

Habit energies are the basis of internal knots. This is like when we put flower petals into tea in order to flavor it. If we are in a good environment, we get the "perfume" of the good environment. If we are in an unwholesome environment, we get the "perfume" of an unwholesome environment. Any action of body, speech, or mind can be the result of a habit energy. Some habit energies have taken thousands of years to form. Our heritage is not only what we have done in the past, but what we are doing in the present. Every word we speak and every act we perform will determine how we are. We know that if we want to come to a place of happiness and light, we must develop good habits. The best habit is the practice of mindfulness. If we live with a Sangha that practices mindfulness, we will get the perfume of mindfulness.

There are two kinds of habit energy. The first is *karma-vasana*, literally, "action perfuming," a habit formed by an action. If we practice walking meditation for three weeks, it will become a habit. Then, when we go to the airport and we have to wait for our flight, we will be able to draw upon the habit energy of walking meditation. Habit energies are our only true belongings, the only heritage we will continue to own when we die. Everything else—our loved ones, our home, our college degrees—we have to leave behind. All we take with us is our karma-vasana, and we can't choose to take only the part of it that we like; we have to take it all. The fifth of the Five Remembrances reminds us of this: "My actions are my only true belongings. I cannot escape the consequences of my actions. My actions are the ground on which I stand."

The second kind of habit energy is *graha-dvaya-vasana*, the habit energy of grasping duality. We have the habit of perceiving phenomena in terms of opposites, thinking that the object exists outside the subject, that there is self and other. When we live in mindfulness we see that the world is just our consciousness, individual and collective, and that self and other, birth and death, coming and going, existence and nonexistence are only notions.

When the two kinds of habit energy are transformed, when the internal knots have been untied, the fruit of the practice reveals itself. This is called transformation at the base (ashraya paravritti). Transformation at the base means transformation in the depths of the store consciousness, because it is the base of all other consciousnesses and ultimately of the entire universe. If we learn, reason, talk about, and accept the theory of nonself, we can make a small transformation in our mind consciousness. But to transform the root, the base, we have to transform the blocks of ignorance in our unconscious mind. If we cannot touch these things, true transformation cannot take place. The practice is not a matter of transforming our intellect alone.

When we are able to touch our habit energies and transform the roots of violence, despair, fear, and anger in our store consciousness, transformation at the base occurs. We begin by recognizing the internal knots and latent tendencies in order to transform them. We have to train ourselves in the way of looking with the insights of nonself and interbeing. Day and night we have to water the seed of understanding in our store consciousness so that it will grow and help us to see the nature of interbeing in everything we see and touch. We have to bring this understanding into our daily life.

47

The Present Moment

The present moment
contains past and future.
The secret of transformation
is in the way we handle this very moment.

THE PRESENT MOMENT contains past and future—this is a teaching from the Avatamsaka Sutra. The one contains the all. Time contains space. When we are in contact with the present moment, we are in contact with all time, including the past and future. Since time also contains space, the present moment also contains this place and all other places. Standing on the Earth's surface, dwelling in the present moment, the ground under our feet is boundless. Standing in Paris, we see that we are standing on the whole of Europe. And if we remain firmly and solidly in the present moment, we see that we are also standing on Asia, the Americas, Africa, and the whole Earth. In the present moment, we are able to touch the whole world and the whole universe.

How we handle the present moment is the key to transforming suffering. This is an essential teaching of Buddhism. Western psychology takes a different approach. Psychoanalysis works by opening the door to the past and touching what happened there. According to this method, our suffering is the result of unresolved conflicting tendencies in us. These internal knots—anger, hatred, fear, anxiety—have been in our mind since childhood. Because our conscious mind was unable to bear the pain of these conflicts as they were occurring, it buried them deeply in our unconscious, and ever since our conscious mind has tried to keep these unbearable anxieties from entering its territory. So these painful memories remain in the unconscious, always looking for ways to surface. From time to time they emerge in one form or another. We do, say, or think things that are surprising to us, that seem out of proportion to the immediate situation. The lack of peace and joy in the unconscious mind leads to these abnormal outward expressions.

Freud proposed that when we shine the light of the conscious mind into the dark corners of the unconscious mind, our psychological sickness slowly lessens. The methodology he developed is for the patient to sit or lie down on a comfortable couch while the analyst sits behind him, where he cannot be seen. This is so that the patient will not feel shy or embarrassed to say whatever comes to mind. The patient is lying down, relaxed, with his arms at his sides, allowing his brain the freedom to make images. Whatever images occur to him, he tells the analyst. From time to time, the analyst may say something to encourage the patient to speak. The analyst may suggest that he recall a specific memory from childhood. As the patient talks about his childhood, certain details emerge from his unconscious mind without him recognizing their importance. The analyst notes these details and may ask questions to explore these areas further.

The analyst may ask his patient to tell him about a recent dream. According to psychoanalysis, dreams are the road to the unconscious mind. Or he might ask the patient to recount something that happened recently, something painful or remarkable, a failure or an awkward moment. Talking about these things, the patient will, from time to time, reveal images bubbling up from the unconscious. A well-trained analyst will be able to read the images lying in the patient's unconscious mind. Together, analyst and patient delve into the past and contact these thoughts and images buried in the depths of the patient's consciousness that are causing him to suffer in the present moment. Essential to this process is that the patient be relaxed, not consciously thinking about anything. He lets himself be quite natural and when something comes into his mind he tells the analyst, because he has confidence that the analyst can help him.

This might sound easy, but it is not. Thoughts and images often appear in our mind that we don't have the courage to say out loud. When we talk, we usually edit ourselves, but this does not help us see the truth. In the psychoanalytic model, only when we have confidence in the analyst do we feel relaxed and natural and start to tell the whole truth. The more we tell, the more material the analyst has to help us see and be in contact with our unconscious mind.

Freud is regarded as the first Western psychologist to discover the unconscious. The influence of this discovery on the literature, philosophy, and psychology of the West has been considerable. Freud noticed there were people suffering from deafness, dumbness, blindness, and paralysis who had nothing physically wrong with their optic, aural, or motor nervous systems. He then tried hypnosis and found that patients could say things they were unable to recall when not in the hypnotic state. Freud concluded that the physical symptoms of the illness were arising from the mind, not from physiological disorders. This led to Freud's "discovery" of the unconscious.

Sometimes five- or six-year-old children become deaf when their parents' hostile conversations cause the child unbearable suffering. Sometimes people go blind to avoid seeing things that cause them to suffer. A person's hand can become paralyzed because they were coerced to use their hand to gratify someone's sexual desire. Psychoanalysis aims at uncovering this buried knowledge about the past to explain our present suffering. Its emphasis is on the past as the key to the present.

Humanistic psychology, a later branch of the Western psychological tradition, says that we do not need to go into the past; we need to give more attention to the present. Carl Rogers, one of the leading figures of humanistic psychology, proposed the following five guidelines:

1) We should give primary importance to the present instead of to the past;

2) When there is a feeling, we should give our attention to that feeling rather than looking for its source in the past;

3) We should use the raw materials of the conscious mind rather than the raw materials of the unconscious mind;

4) We should assume immediate responsibility for whatever arises in the sphere of our feelings, and;

5) If we give our attention to making our life peaceful and joyful now, quite naturally our illness will lessen.

Buddhist psychology contains elements of both these approaches. Buddhism sees all the information in the mind consciousness as coming from the unconscious mind, the store consciousness. Seeds of suffering in the store consciousness, when manifested in mind consciousness, create more suffering. Freud's notion of the unconscious as the key to suffering is similar, except in its emphasis on examining past events—which have sown the seeds of suffering in the store consciousness—rather than transforming their manifestation as mental formations in the present.

As we learned in Verse Forty-Five, Buddhist practice offers three methods of treating suffering that comes from seeds of past suffering. First, we get in contact with what is healthy, refreshing, and beautiful in the present; second, we practice mindfulness to recognize the painful feelings as they arise; and third, when we are ready, we invite the painful feelings up into our mind consciousness where we can touch them with our mindfulness and transform them. All three of these methods focus on the present moment, because the past and the present inter-are. The present already contains the past. This is the truth of interbeing. Through the energy of mindfulness we recognize what is happening in the present moment and we are able to discover its basis.

When irritation or despair arises in us, first of all we have to take responsibility for it. I have the greatest responsibility for my anger, but my brother also has some responsibility for it. It was he who said the words that watered the seeds of anger in my store consciousness. My sister, too, has some responsibility, because my anger has a collective nature and she is also part of the collective, even though she has not said or done anything to water those seeds.

All phenomena have an individual and a collective nature. Suffering is not only an individual manifestation but a collective manifestation from many generations and from society. There is no one, therefore, who is not co-responsible for what takes place in me. The responsibility is more or less, according to the person and circumstances. And, by the same token, I am co-responsible for what takes place in those around me.

It is very useful for us to take responsibility for what is happening in our mind. We are ninety percent responsible for our anger, so we don't blame others, even if they played a direct or indirect part in bringing about our anger. Rather than waste time searching for reasons for our anger, we instead use our energy to take care of it. When a feeling of suffering arises, we embrace it with the energy of mindfulness. We do this for all our ancestors as well as for future generations.

The basic method of healing is to be mindful of refreshing and beautiful things in the present moment. This simple method is not as well known, celebrated, and widely practiced as it could be. It is easy to take joy and peace for granted. When everything is running smoothly, no one says anything about it. When someone smiles beautifully, it is not printed in the newspaper. But when someone gets so angry that he kills another person, that is considered news.

With the first method, we are not consciously healing ourselves; healing takes place indirectly. There are also direct forms of healing. The Manifestation Only teachings say that it is possible not only to use mindfulness to recognize our suffering as it arises so that it becomes less strong, but we can then invite it into our conscious mind in order to transform it directly. In this way, these teachings go further than the humanistic psychology approach.

The roots of our suffering and ignorance can all be found in our store consciousness, the base, in the present moment. So the intelligent thing to do is to make the present moment beautiful and fresh, to transform it. It isn't necessary to say, "We have to suffer today in order to have peace and joy tomorrow," or "This is not my real home, I will wait until I am in paradise to be happy." We want to take care of the future. But the future will be made of only one substance: the present moment. The best way to take care of the future is to do our best to take care of the present moment. It isn't helpful to get lost in the past or future. When we are lost, we cannot take care of the present, the past, or the future. The secret of transformation at the base lies in our handling of this very moment with mindfulness. If we know how to handle the present moment, not only will we live deeply each moment of our life, but we can also transform the past and build a future.

Dwelling in the present moment does not prevent us from looking into the past or the future. Grounded in the present, we can survey the past or look to the future and learn a lot, but it isn't helpful to get lost in them. The secret of transformation at the base lies in our handling of this very moment. We have to practice mindfulness in every moment. If we know how to touch deeply the present moment, we can also touch and even change the past. In the past I might have made a mistake and made someone suffer. The scar of suffering is still in me, and it is still in the other person as well. With the energy of mindfulness I can recognize the wound in myself, and I can say to the person I harmed, "I'm sorry, I will never do that again." My parents and grandparents are still there in the past, whether manifested or not manifested. If we make ourself truly present in the here and the now, we can see them smiling to us.

The determination to begin anew is a very powerful energy. It can help begin to heal our wounds right away and relieve our suffering and the suffering of others. We can help many people be liberated from their guilt by offering them this kind of teaching and practice.

The Discourse on Living Happily in the Present Moment is the most ancient teaching on this subject.[36] The Buddha said many times that his teaching was to help people to have peace and joy in the present moment, which would guarantee not only their present happiness but their future happiness as well. If the present can be joyful, the future can also be joyful. The Sanskrit phrase, "*Drishta-dharma-sukha-viharin,*" sums this up. *Drishta* means what can be seen, touched, and realized in the present moment. Dharma means phenomena. *Sukha* means happiness. *Viharin* means abiding. "Touching the present moment, we abide in happiness." There are always enough internal and external conditions to make us happy in the present moment.

This is not to deny that there are also elements of suffering in us and around us. But the elements of suffering do not remove the elements of happiness. If we touch only suffering elements, we are not really living. Some people become imprisoned in their suffering. Wherever they look, they see what is wrong, what is hurtful. They may know in principle that the flower is beautiful and the sunset is majestic, but they are not able to touch them. There is a wall surrounding them that prevents them from being in contact with the flower, the sunset, and all the wonders of the natural world and the present moment that are always available to them. If these people could touch the healthy and beautiful things that lie within

36 See Thich Nhat Hanh, *Our Appointment with Life: Discourse on Living Happily in the Present Moment* (Berkeley, CA: Parallax Press, 1990).

them and around them, their suffering would decrease. It is not enough to touch our suffering. We have to be in touch with the healthy and wonderful things in life as well. To do this, we need a Sangha, a group of friends, who smile, share with us, understand us, and take steps with us in freedom to help pull us out of our world of darkness.

If a feeling of suffering arises, we embrace it with the energy of mindfulness. We do that for all our ancestors and for future generations. The suffering is not only an individual manifestation, but a collective manifestation from many generations and from society. We are not the only one responsible.

48

Sangha

Transformation takes place
in our daily life.
To make the work of transformation easy,
practice with a Sangha.

THE VERSE REFERS to the practice in daily life and to the community that supports our practice, the Sangha. Sometimes we think it might be easier to live and practice alone, to live on a mountaintop and close the door to our private hut. Actually, practicing on our own is much more difficult. We humans are social animals, and our joys and hopes depend on being with others.

Our practice is simple: mindfulness in our daily life. We practice the meditation techniques of stopping and looking deeply. We do this to keep from being pulled along in many directions. Practice helps us to stop running headlong through our lives as though Mara himself were chasing us. Too often we are carried along by the energy of the people around us, by circumstances, by our own thoughts, by anger, and we don't have the strength to go against these forces. Ask yourself, "What have I done with my life over the past few years?" If you have not practiced stopping, the years will seem to have gone by in a dream. You may never have stopped for a moment to look at the moon or hold a flower in your hands. Without stopping and looking deeply, we are not able to really live our lives.

The energy that enables us to stop is mindfulness. We can use the things that are already present in our lives—the ringing of the telephone, the time spent stopped at a red light when driving—to help us remember to stop, breathe, smile, and come back to the present moment. The sound of the telephone is the voice of the Buddha calling us back to our true self, asking,

"Where are you going? Why don't you come back home?" We are like children who have run away from home. Hearing the sound of the telephone, we can come back to the here and now. The present moment is filled with joy, peace, freedom, and awakening. We only have to stop and touch it.

The practice of stopping brings concentration (samadhi). Concentration makes our mindfulness more stable. If the battery in our flashlight is fully charged, the light will be strong and stable and we'll be able to see any object we shine it on clearly. But if the battery is weak, we'll only see a vague, flickering image. Concentration is the battery; the flashlight is mindfulness. When we stop and concentrate our minds even a little, we begin to see. If we stop for longer, the energy of concentration in us becomes very strong, and wherever we shine the light of our mindfulness, we can see clearly. With concentration, looking deeply (vipashyana) is much easier. In fact, concentration and looking deeply cannot be separated. As soon as there is concentration, looking deeply is already there. For there to be looking deeply, there must first be stopping. When we stop and look deeply into a flower, we can see its interdependent co-arising nature, the sun, rain, and soil in the flower.

We can practice concentration and looking deeply in all the activities of our daily life. Even while walking, we can practice stopping. We walk in a way that does not make arriving the only goal. We walk to enjoy each step. If we practice stopping while sweeping the floor, washing the dishes, or taking a shower, we are living deeply. If we do not practice this way, the days and months will flow by and we will be wasting our time. Stopping helps us live authentically.

Even though the practice is simple it can be difficult to maintain by ourselves in isolation. The forces that pull us along are strong. But if we are part of a community, a Sangha, where everyone is practicing this way, it becomes simple and natural. The Sangha is a community in which everyone has the intention to learn and practice. But good intentions are not enough. We have to learn the art of living happily together.

Sangha-building is the most important work of the practice. We need to learn the art of forming a community that is happy and gives people a feeling of confidence. A practice center should be organized like a family. The teacher is like a father or mother. Senior practitioners are like elder brothers or sisters, uncles and aunts. If a practice center is not organized as a spiritual family where everyone feels like a valued member, the work of transformation is difficult. Many people come to the practice from broken homes and a troubled society. If the practice center is organized in such a way that everyone is an island, without much contact, affection, or warmth from other members, even if they were to practice for ten or twenty years, there will be no fruit. We need to put down roots. Without roots, it is difficult to function happily.

A teacher is also helped by a good Sangha. However brilliant a teacher may be, unless he or she is part of a Sangha, there is not much they can do. A teacher without a Sangha is like a manufacturer without materials or a musician without an instrument. The capacity of a teacher can be seen in the quality of his or her community. If there is harmony in the Sangha, even a short-term visitor to the community will receive some benefit.

Do not expect any teacher or Sangha to be perfect. We need only a committed group of ordinary people in order to receive great benefit from it. When the individuals in the group take refuge in the Sangha, it will grow strong and beautiful. When we smile and take a conscious breath, our whole Sangha is smiling and taking a conscious breath with us. In a Sangha, there is mutual helping. When we fall down, there is always someone who can help us up. When we practice walking meditation, we are serving our Sangha. The techniques for building a Sangha are the half-smile, walking meditation, stopping (shamatha), and abiding in the present moment. When we build on these foundations, we can help others. Most important is that the Sangha be happy, nurturing, and stable.

The best way to help build such a Sangha is to be a wholesome element in your own practice community. A Sangha is where you can receive and participate in the tradition. But it does not just spring up on its own. It is what we ourselves make. There are those who want to take refuge in the Buddha and the Dharma, but not the Sangha. Others want to take refuge only in the Sangha of great cosmic bodhisattvas such as Shariputra, Maudgalyayana, Samantabhadra, and Manjushri, not in the ordinary practitioners living in their own community. We take refuge in the Buddha as a result of having confidence in the teachings and practice. The Buddha is mindfulness. He shows the way to go. But taking refuge in the Sangha is not a matter of mere belief. It is an expression of our confidence based on our experience of practicing in a community.

Transformation takes place in our daily life. Taking refuge in and practicing with a Sangha is very important. Don't wait to build a Sangha. Learn to live in harmony and happiness now and build your Sangha right here in the present moment. Practicing without a Sangha is difficult. Not only monks and nuns but all practitioners need a Sangha for support. When you practice with a Sangha, the fruits of the practice are easily obtained. When you take refuge in a Sangha, the work of transformation will be realized.

We should also understand Sangha as environment. Transformation and healing are not easy without an appropriate environment. In a good, healthy environment the positive elements in us will be touched and will manifest, and the negative elements will diminish and will recede to the background. This principle is applied to both mental and physical conditions. In the light of interbeing, a seed is made of all the seeds, and a gene is made of all the genes, embracing within itself all wholesome and unwholesome elements, like a computer that has the capacity of accessing all the information on the internet. When one type of information appears on the screen, all other information will have to be latent, in the background. We can choose to keep the manifested materials as long as we wish and prevent other information from coming to the foreground. A good environment is so crucial for the work of transformation and healing. A good seed or a good gene can be planted, but if a good environment is not there, then the good seed or gene will not be able to stay long in the foreground. This is why Sangha-building and the setting up of healthy environments should be seen as the most urgent task in our modern society.

Asanga, in his Summary of the Great Vehicle, speaks about the six characteristics of the seeds: momentariness, simultaneity, sequential continuity, determined status, dependence on conditions, and productivity of specific results. The first characteristic (momentariness) confirms the teaching of impermanence: all formations undergo change in every moment. This is to say that transformation and healing are possible. The second characteristic (simultaneity) means seeds inter-are and coexist with the sense organs and their objects—they do not exist separately from consciousness, the subject of cognition, and the object of cognition. A kernel of corn contains the corn plant within itself. Thus the teaching of interbeing is confirmed. The third characteristic (sequential continuity) shows the nature of interaction and inter-production of seeds and formations: seeds manifesting as formations, formations producing and nourishing seeds.

The fourth characteristic (determined status) and the sixth characteristic (productivity of specific results) demonstrate the consistency of causes and effects: a negative formation such as anger produces or strengthens the seed of anger; a positive formation such as compassion produces or strengthens the seed of compassion. But in the light of impermanence and interbeing, both the formation and the seed can change, can be transformed and lose their "determined status." A seed or a formation is defined as unwholesome because the unwholesome elements in them have come and manifested in the foreground, while all the wholesome elements, due to the lack of a good environment, have to be hidden in the background. Since transformation is possible, garbage can become flowers, and afflictions can become enlightenment. Therefore we have to be careful about how to understand these two characteristics put forth by Asanga. As for the fifth characteristic (dependence on conditions), we can understand that if we can provide a good environment and a good Sangha, transformation will occur.

49

Nothing to Attain

Nothing is born, nothing dies.
Nothing to hold on to, nothing to release.
Samsara is nirvana.
There is nothing to attain.

THIS VERSE REFERS to the ultimate dimension: the fruit of the practice, nirvana, going beyond birth and death. But the historical dimension is not separate from the ultimate dimension. We say that we "attain" the ultimate dimension, but we do not attain anything. The wave does not need to attain the state of being water—the wave *is* water. We live in the historical dimension, in the world of existence and nonexistence, continuation and cessation, coming and going—and, at the same time, we are in touch with nirvana. Nirvana is our true nature. Just as a wave has always been water, we have always been in nirvana.

The Three Dharma Seals—impermanence, nonself, and nirvana—are the keys that open the gate of the Fifty Verses. The Three Dharma Seals are like the two sides of a coin and the metal from which it is made. Touching either side of the coin, we touch the metal, the base, at the same time. It is because we think things are permanent and have a separate self that we have ideas about existence and nonexistence, one and many, coming and going, birth and death. By looking into impermanence and nonself we can be in touch with nirvana. Impermanence and nonself refer to phenomena, the wave. Just as we might look into a wave to find out what it is made of, we look into the impermanent and selfless nature of all that is and, in doing so, we are able to go beyond ideas of existence and nonexistence, one and many, coming and going, birth and death. This is nirvana, the extinction of all ideas and notions, including ideas about impermanence and nonself. Impermanence and nonself are ideas designed to help us go beyond the ideas of permanence and self. But they are ideas nonetheless—fabrications, not reality. Nirvana transcends the notions of permanence and impermanence.

From the point of view of the three natures, the nature of imaginary construction views things as permanent and having a self. In the light of Interdependent Co-Arising, we see the nature of things as impermanent and without self. Looking in this way releases us from the imaginary constructed nature and helps us be in contact with the fulfilled nature. When we touch the wave, we touch the water. And finally, when we touch impermanence, we touch nirvana. That is why there is nothing for us to attain. There is nothing to hold on to and nothing to release. Everything is already present.

We get caught by ideas of birth and death. We think that to be born means that from nothing we become something and from no one we become someone. We believe that to die means that from being someone we become no one, from something we become nothing. But looking deeply, we see that these notions cannot be applied to reality. There is no birth and no death, only continuation.

When the cloud is transformed into rain and falls in the river, the ocean, and on the land, it does not die. It just continues in a different form. As it merges with the stream, it continues to change. It is wonderful to be a cloud floating in the sky. But it is also wonderful to be rain falling on a field. A sheet of paper cannot be reduced to nothingness. Even if you burn it, it will still continue in other forms. Some of it will rise as smoke into the sky and become part of a cloud. Some will become the energy of heat. Some will become ash falling to the ground, merging with the earth. A few weeks from now this paper may manifest as a tiny flower in the grass. Will we be able to recognize its presence? Nothing dies. You cannot reduce something to nothing.

There is a famous Zen koan: What was your face before you were born? Contemplating this is meant to help us realize the no-birth, no-death nature of reality and of ourselves. The eighteenth-century French scientist Antoine Laurent Lavoisier said, "Nothing is born. Nothing dies." He was not a Buddhist but a scientist looking deeply into the nature of reality, and he discovered this truth. The Heart Sutra also says, "No birth, no death, no production, no destruction." If you have never been born, how can you die? Grasping and rejecting are only possible when you have not seen into the heart of reality.

We usually try to hold onto life and run away from death. But, according to the teaching, everything has been nirvana from the non-beginning. So why do we have to grasp one thing and avoid another? In the ultimate dimension, there is no beginning and no end. We think there is something to attain, something outside of ourselves, but everything is already here. When we transcend notions of inside and outside, we know that the object we wish to attain is already within us. We don't have to search for it in space or time. It is already available in the present moment. The contemplation on non-attainment is very important. The object we wish to attain already is attained. We don't need to attain anything. We already have it. We already are it.

The teaching of non-attainment is developed from the teaching of aimlessness. The teaching of the Three Doors of Liberation is common to all the Buddhist schools. The first door is emptiness. Everything is empty. Empty of what? Empty of a separate self. A flower is full of everything in the cosmos—sunshine, clouds, air, and space. It is empty of only one thing, a separate existence. That is the meaning of emptiness. We can use this as a key to unlock the door to reality.

The second door is signlessness. If you see a flower only as a flower and don't see the sunshine, clouds, earth, time, and space in it, you are caught in the sign of the flower. But when you have touched the nature of interbeing of the flower, you truly see the flower. If you see a person and don't also see his society, education, ancestors, culture, and environment, you have not really seen that person. Instead, you have been taken in by the sign of that person, the outward appearance of a separate self. When you can see that person deeply, you touch the whole cosmos and you will not be fooled by appearances. This is called signlessness.

The third door is aimlessness. We already are what we want to become. We don't have to become someone else. All we have to do is be ourselves, fully and authentically. We don't have to run after anything. We already contain the whole cosmos. We simply return to ourselves through mindfulness and touch the peace and joy that are already present within us and all around us. I have arrived. I am already home. There is nothing to do. This is the third key for unlocking reality. Aimlessness, non-attainment, is a wonderful practice.

Our afflictions are none other than enlightenment. We can ride the waves of birth and death in peace. We can travel in the boat of compassion on the ocean of delusion with a smile of non-fear. In the light of interbeing, we see the flower in the garbage and the garbage in the flower. It is on the very ground of suffering, the ground of afflictions, that we can contemplate enlightenment and well-being. It is exactly in the muddy water that the lotus grows and blooms.

Bodhisattvas are those who have penetrated into the reality of no birth and no death. That is why they are fearless, day and night. With that freedom, they can do a lot to help those who are suffering. We can become a Buddha only by being in the world of suffering and afflictions. And when we are free, we can ride on the waves of birth and death without fear, helping those who are drowning in the ocean of suffering.

50

No Fear

When we realize that afflictions are no other than enlightenment,
we can ride the waves of birth and death in peace,
traveling in the boat of compassion on the ocean of delusion,
smiling the smile of non-fear.

THE FINAL VERSE of the Fifty Verses describes the bodhisattva, an enlightened being who instead of entering nirvana and leaving behind the cycle of suffering, chooses to stay in the world of birth and death to help others. Bodhisattvas dwell on the same ground as the rest of us—the world of birth and death, permanence, and self. But thanks to the practice of looking deeply into impermanence and nonself, they are in touch with the ultimate dimension, free from the fears associated with ideas of existence and nonexistence, one and many, coming and going, birth and death. In this freedom, they ride the waves of birth and death in perfect peace. They are able to remain in the world of waves while abiding in the nature of water.

"Riding the waves of birth and death" is a description of the bodhisattvas in the Lotus Sutra—Avalokiteshvara, Samantabhadra, Bhaishajyaraja, and Gadgadasvara—who demonstrate the practice in this life. This is the dimension of action. In a world of pain and grief, these bodhisattvas are still able to smile with compassion and fearlessness, because they are able to see the nonduality of afflictions and awakening and touch the reality of nirvana.

Buddhist texts speak of three kinds of gifts—material resources, sharing the Dharma with others, and non-fear, which is the greatest gift. Because bodhisattvas are free from fear, they can help many people. Non-fear is the greatest gift we can offer to those we love. Nothing is more precious. But we cannot offer that gift unless we ourselves have it. If we have practiced and have touched the ultimate dimension of reality, we too can smile the bodhisattvas' smile of non-fear. Like them, we don't need to run away from our afflictions. We don't need to go somewhere else to attain enlightenment. We see that afflictions and enlightenment are one. When we have a deluded mind, we see only afflictions. But when we have a true mind, the afflictions are no longer there. There is only enlightenment. We are no longer afraid of birth and death because we have touched the nature of interbeing.

Those who work with the dying especially need to practice solidity and non-fear. Others need our stability and non-fear in order to be able to die peacefully. If we know how to touch the ultimate dimension of reality, if we know the reality of no birth and no death, we can transcend all fear. Then, when we are sitting with a dying person, we can be a source of comfort and inspiration to them. Non-fear is the greatest practice in Buddhism. To free ourselves from all fear we must touch the ground of our being and train ourselves to look directly into the light of compassion.

The Heart Sutra describes how the bodhisattva Avalokiteshvara, because he is able to look deeply into the nonself nature of the Five Aggregates, discovers the nature of emptiness and immediately overcomes all afflictions.[37] From this he receives the energy of non-fear, which is why he is able to help so many others. Once we have seen that our afflictions are no other than enlightenment, we too can ride joyfully on the waves of birth and death.

A gardener does not chase after flowers and try to run away from garbage. She accepts both, and she takes good care of both. She is not attached to either nor does she reject either, because she sees that the nature of both is interbeing. She has made peace with the flower and the garbage. A bodhisattva handles enlightenment and afflictions in the same way a skillful gardener handles flowers and garbage—without discrimination. She knows how to do the work of transformation, and so she is no longer afraid. This is the attitude of a Buddha.

37 See Thich Nhat Hanh, *Our Appointment with Life: Discourse on Living Happily in the Present Moment.*

Afterword
The Sources of the Fifty Verses

THE DEVELOPMENT of Indian Buddhist philosophy and doctrine is generally divided into three periods, Original Buddhism, Many-Schools Buddhism, and Mahayana Buddhism.[38] The Fifty Verses contain elements from the teachings of all three periods.

The Abhidharma ("Super Dharma") is a primary text of Original Buddhism. One hundred and forty years after the Buddha's parinirvana ("great passing away"), the Sangha underwent a division into two streams, Sthaviravada and the Mahasanghika.[39] This marked the transition into the Many-Schools period, when eighteen or twenty new schools came into being, due in most cases to disputes about various points of doctrine.[40] From the Sthaviravada there later arose two sects, the Sarvastivada and the Sautrantika. The other main branch of Many-Schools Buddhism, the Mahasanghika, was one of the progenitors of the third great phase of Indian Buddhism, the Mahayana (literally, "Great Vehicle").[41]

38 These three periods date from the time of the Buddha in the mid-sixth to mid-fifth century B.C.E. to about the seventh century C.E. For a general outline, see Thich Nhat Hanh, *The Heart of the Buddha's Teaching*, Chapter 4.

39 Here the term Sangha is used in its most restrictive sense, meaning the community of ordained Buddhist monastics. However, in modern usage and throughout the rest of the book, it refers to the community of Buddhist followers in general. The Sthaviras were the progenitors of the Theravada school (literally, "Way of the Elders"), the primary form of Buddhism found today in South and Southeast Asia.

40 For a detailed description of the various schools and their doctrinal differences see Edward Conze, *Buddhist Thought in India* (Ann Arbor, MI: Ann Arbor Paperbacks/University of Michigan Press, 1967, 1987).

41 The Mahayana developed from the first century B.C.E. to the first century C.E. Mahayanists proposed the ideal of the bodhisattva (literally, "enlightening being"), who works toward the

During his lifetime the Buddha was the living Dharma, but after he died his disciples were left with the task of systematizing his teachings so that they could be further studied. The Abhidharma was the first such collection, but this work continued through the centuries as Buddhist philosophy was further developed and expanded upon. In the fifth century C.E., Buddhaghosa composed a popular work of systemization, The Path of Purification (Visuddhimagga).[42] Around the same time, the great monk-scholar Vasubandhu compiled a summary and commentary of the Buddha's teachings called the Treasury of the Abidharma (Abhidharma-kosha- bhashya).[43]

Vasubandhu practiced with a number of Buddhist schools around Gandhara in what is now North Pakistan. Then he went north to Kashmir, the center of the Sarvastivada school (which formed the basis of much of early Chinese Buddhism). The Sarvastivadins allowed only Kashmiris to study and practice with them, however, so Vasubandhu disguised himself in order to receive their teachings. After completing his studies with the Sarvastivadins, Vasubandhu composed the Abhidharma-kosha-bhashya. His teachers saw that he had a great understanding of the teachings of their tradition, but they didn't realize that the Abhidharma-kosha-bhashya also included teachings from the Sautrantika and other schools.

Vasubandhu had a half-brother, Asanga, who was an accomplished Mahayana Buddhist monk and scholar. He composed an important treatise on the Abhidharma from a Mahayana perspective, the Mahayana-samgraha-shastra.[44] Asanga often spoke to Vasubandhu of the significance of the Mahayana teachings, but Vasubandhu remained skeptical. He appreci-

---

awakening of all beings, in contrast to the early Buddhist ideal of the arhat (literally, "worthy one") who focuses on his or her own liberation. Mahayana Buddhism is the most prominent form of Buddhism in China, Tibet, Korea, Japan, and most of Vietnam.

42 Buddhaghosa, *The Path of Purification (Visuddhimagga)*. Translated by Bhikkhu Ñanamoli, Third Edition (Kandy, Sri Lanka: Buddhist Publication Society, 1975).

43 Translated into English from Louis de la Vallée Poussin's French translation by Leo Pruden, *Abhidharma Kosha Bhashya* (Fremont, CA: Asian Humanities Press, imprint of Jain Publishing Company, 1990).

44 *Samgraha* means compendium, summary, or essence. A *shastra* is a commentary. This text has been translated into French by Étienne Lamotte, *La Somme du Grand Véhicule d'Asanga* (Louvain, Belgium: Institut Orientaliste, Éditions Peeters, 1973); and into English by John P. Keenan, *The Summary of the Great Vehicle* (Berkeley, CA: Numata Center for Buddhist Translation and Research, 1992).

ated the teachings and practice of the Many-Schools tradition, but he felt that later developments, including the Mahayana, were not authentic Buddhism. Then one full-moon night, as Vasubandhu was practicing walking meditation, he came across Asanga standing by a clear pond chanting Mahayana teachings. Suddenly, Vasubandhu had a breakthrough into the depth and beauty of the Great Vehicle and from that moment on the two brothers practiced and taught Mahayana Buddhism together.

Vasubandhu is regarded as the patriarch and most outstanding figure of the Vijñaptimatra or Manifestation Only school, which grew out of the Yogachara school of Mahayana Buddhism.[45] He wrote commentaries on Asanga's work and he also composed two seminal treatises on the teachings of the Manifestation Only school, the Twenty Verses on the Manifestation of Consciousness (*Vijñaptimatrata-vimshatika-karika*) and the Thirty Verses on the Manifestation of Consciousness (*Vijñaptimatrata-trimshika-karika*).[46]

Because of Vasubandhu's training in several traditions, we can see how the Manifestation Only school developed from the Abhidharma of the Sarvastivada school and from Vasubandhu's own work, the Abhidharma-

45 Both Vijñanavada and Yogachara were early Mahayana Buddhist schools based on the study of the nature of consciousness. Vijñana means literally "mind" or "consciousness"; the school is more commonly referred to as the Mind Only or Consciousness Only school. This name is often misunderstood as a kind of idealism, however, so throughout this book I refer to it as the Manifestation Only (Vijñaptimatra) school. The Yogachara (literally, "application of yoga") school derives its name from its emphasis on the practice of "yoga," meaning meditation, particularly the meditative practices of the perfections (paramitas), the essential qualities of a bodhisattva.

46 *Vimshatika* means "twenty"; *trimshika* means "thirty." *Vijñapti* means "manifestation"; *matra* means "only." *Vijñaptimatra* is thus "manifestation only." *Karika* is a verse that expresses a teaching concisely. These two treatises appear in a French translation, *Deux Traités de Vasubandhu: Vimshatika et Trimshika*, translated into French by Sylvain Lévi (Paris: Bibliothèque de l'École des Hautes Études, 1925) and into English by many scholars, including David J. Kalupahana, in *The Principles of Buddhist Psychology* (Albany, NY: State University of New York Press, 1987), pp. 173–92; and Francis H. Cook, in *Three Texts on Consciousness Only* (Berkeley, CA: Numata Center for Buddhist Translation and Research, 1999), "Thirty Verses on Consciousness Only" (pp. 371–83), and "The Treatise in Twenty Verses on Consciousness Only" (pp. 385–408). A Sanskrit version of the *Thirty Verses* was discovered by Professor Sylvain Lévi in the 1920s. A translation from Vasubandhu's original Sanskrit to Chinese by Xuanzang, along with Xuanzang's commentary, is also extant. The original Sanskrit to Tibetan has been translated into English by Stefan Anacker in his *Seven Works of Vasubandhu: The Buddhist Psychological Doctor* (Delhi: Motilal Banarsidass, 1984, 1998), pp. 181–190.

kosha-bhashya, which he wrote before coming into contact with the Mahayana. Thus the Manifestation Only school contains many elements of non-Mahayana teachings. Vasubandhu's writings have served the Great Vehicle deeply and effectively, but they never became one hundred percent Mahayana. Two centuries after his time, the Manifestation Only school was still regarded as an "interim vehicle."[47]

In the seventh century, the Chinese Buddhist monk Xuanzang (600–664), known as "The Pilgrim," traveled to India and attended Nalanda University, the principal seat of Buddhist studies. In his chronicles of his travels in Central Asia and India, Xuanzang observed that ten thousand monks were studying at Nalanda.[48] Under the guidance of the master Shilabhadra, Xuanzang studied Manifestation Only Buddhism. Shilabhadra, then one hundred years old, was Nalanda's rector and the last of the ten illustrious "doctors" of the Manifestation Only school (Vasubandhu was the first. Another was Sthiramati.[49] Dharmapala, Shilabhadra's teacher, was the ninth).

Comparing the texts of Sthiramati and Dharmapala, we can see how their approaches to Manifestation Only differ. Vasubandhu's original commentary was also added to by Dignaga, who incorporated elements of epistemology and logic into it. This mélange was the teaching that Xuanzang studied at Nalanda and later continued to study after he returned to China. He founded a school based on the teachings of the manifestation of consciousness, the Wei Shi ("Consciousness Only") school, and wrote a commentary on Vasubandhu's Thirty Verses entitled the Standard Verses on

47 The Japanese Buddhist scholar Takakusu refers to it as "semi-Mahayanistic" and "quasi-Mahayanistic" in *Essentials of Buddhist Philosophy* (Honolulu, HI: University of Hawaii Press, 1947).

48 Nalanda University, founded in the fifth century, was located about five miles north of Rajagriha, present-day Rajgir, in the north-central Indian state of Bihar. Xuanzang's account of his travels in India has been translated into English by Li Rongxi, *The Great Tang Dynasty Record of the Western Regions* (Berkeley, CA: Numata Center for Buddhist Translation and Research, 1996).

49 Sylvain Lévi also discovered a manuscript in Sanskrit of a commentary by Sthiramati on Vasubandhu's Thirty Verses and published a French translation, *Matériaux pour l'Étude du Système Vijñaptimatra*, edited by Honoré Champion (Paris: Librairie Ancienne, 1932). The French version was subsequently translated into English and this English version has been translated into Chinese.

the Eight Consciousnesses.[50] Xuanzang also put forward the idea of "three realms" of perception, a system that describes the qualities of perception that correspond to different levels of consciousness. He wrote a short poem on the three realms of perception, "The Nature of the Perceived in Itself When Not According to Our Mind," which is included in Chapter Twenty-Four of the Fifty Verses.

A decade after Xuanzang, the Chinese monk Fazang attempted to present the Manifestation Only teachings in a completely Mahayana way. Fazang was a student of the Avatamsaka Sutra (Flower Ornament Discourse) and his important work, The Wondrous Meaning of the Avatamsaka, uses Flower Ornament teachings, especially the notion of "one is all, all is one," to reinforce the teachings of Manifestation Only.[51] But Fazang's efforts were not long-lasting, and no one has continued the work of presenting the Manifestation Only teachings from a Mahayana viewpoint since his time. Even today, scholars and practitioners read the Thirty Verses without taking these important Mahayana Buddhist teachings into account.

The Fifty Verses here are my attempt to continue to polish the precious gems offered by the Buddha, Vasubandhu, Sthiramati, Xuanzang, Fazang, and others. After reading these Fifty Verses, if you are interested in knowing more, you may want to read and understand the classic works of these great masters.

50 This text as such is not found in the *Taisho Tripitaka*, but is included in a commentary on it by Xuanzang's disciple Putai, entitled *Pa-shih Kuei-chu Pu-chu* (Taisho 45, 567–76). Xuanzang's magnum opus is his commentary on Vasubandhu's Thirty Verses, the *Cheng Wei Shi Lun*, which is the foundational text of the Wei Shi (Consciousness Only) school of Chinese Buddhism. This text, along with Vasubandhu's Thirty Verses and Twenty Verses (see note 47, above) has been translated into English by Francis H. Cook and published under the title "Demonstration of Consciousness Only" in *Three Texts on Consciousness Only* (Berkeley, CA: Numata Center for Buddhist Translation and Research, 1999), pp. 7–370.

51 For more on the Avatamsaka Sutra, see Thich Nhat Hanh, *Cultivating the Mind of Love* (Berkeley, CA: Parallax Press, 1996). See also Thomas Cleary, *The Flower Ornament Scripture: A Translation of t he Avatamsaka Sutra* (Boston, MA: Shambhala Publications, 1993), and Cleary's *Entry into the Inconceivable* (Honolulu, HI: University of Hawaii Press, 1983), pp. 147–170.

Dharmcharya Shantum Seth, ordained by Thich Nhat Hanh, offers teachings and shares the practice of Mindf ulness in different parts of India and the world. He also leads pilgrimages 'In the Footsteps of the Buddha'. Please visit: www.buddhapath.com

Practitioners of Mindfulness Meditation meet regularly at different locations in India to meditate and deepen their understanding of the Dharma. Please visit: www.ahimsatrust.org If you would like to attend please write to ahimsa.trust@gmail,com

For worldwide contacts and teachings of Thich Nhat Hanh, Please visit www.plumvillage.org